I0413217

Assessing Survival of Mid-Columbia River Released Juvenile Salmonids at McNary Dam, Washington, 2008–09

By Scott D. Evans, Christopher E. Walker, Scott J. Brewer, and Noah S. Adams

Prepared in cooperation with the U.S. Army Corps of Engineers

Open-File Report 2010-1237

U.S. Department of the Interior
U.S. Geological Survey

U.S. Department of the Interior
KEN SALAZAR, Secretary

U.S. Geological Survey
Marcia K. McNutt, Director

U.S. Geological Survey, Reston, Virginia: 2010

For more information on the USGS—the Federal source for science about the Earth, its natural and living resources, natural hazards, and the environment, visit http://www.usgs.gov or call 1-888-ASK-USGS.

For an overview of USGS information products, including maps, imagery, and publications, visit *http://www.usgs.gov/pubprod*

To order this and other USGS information products, visit *http://store.usgs.gov*

Contents

Figures

iv

Tables

Conversion Factors, Datums, Abbreviations, and Acronyms

Conversion Factors

Inch/Pound to SI

Multiply	By	To obtain
Flow rate		
cubic foot per second (ft^3/s)	0.02832	cubic meter per second (m^3/s)

SI to Inch/Pound

Multiply	By	To obtain
Length		
millimeter (mm)	0.03937	inch (in.)
meter (m)	3.281	foot (ft)
kilometer (km)	0.6214	mile (mi)
Volume		
cubic meter (m^3)	264.2	gallon (gal)
cubic meter (m^3)	35.31	cubic foot (ft^3)
cubic meter (m^3)	1.308	cubic yard (yd^3)
Flow rate		
meter per hour (m/hr)	3.281	foot per hour (ft/hr)
meter per day (m/d)	3.281	foot per day (ft/d)
kilometer per hour (km/h)	0.6214	mile per hour (mi/h)
Mass		
gram (g)	0.03527	ounce, avoirdupois (oz)

Temperature in degrees Celsius (°C) may be converted to degrees Fahrenheit (°F) as follows:
$$°F=(1.8×°C)+32.$$

Datums

Horizontal coordinate information is referenced to the World Geodetic System of 1984 (WGS84).
Vertical coordinate information is referenced to the National Geodetic Vertical Datum of 1929 (NGVD 29).

Abbreviations and Acronyms

ATDL	acoustic tag data loggers	rkm	river kilometers
ATR	acoustic tag receiver	RSSM	route-specific survival model
CJS	Cormack-Jolly-Seber models	TSW	temporary spillway weir
CPUD	Chelan County public utility district	USER	User Specified Estimation Routine
FGE	fish guidance efficiency	USGS	U.S. Geological Survey
FPE	fish passage efficiency		
GPUD	Grant County public utility district		
PIT	passive integrated transponder		
PUD	public utility district		

Assessing Survival of Mid-Columbia River Released Juvenile Salmonids at McNary Dam, Washington, 2008–09

By Scott D. Evans, Christopher E. Walker, Scott J. Brewer, and Noah S. Adams

Abstract

Few studies have evaluated survival of juvenile salmon over long river reaches in the Columbia River and information regarding the survival of sockeye salmon at lower Columbia River dams is lacking. To address these information gaps, the U.S. Geological Survey was contracted by the U.S. Army Corps of Engineers to evaluate the possibility of using tagged fish released in the Mid-Columbia River to assess passage and survival at and downstream of McNary Dam. Using the acoustic telemetry systems already in place for a passage and survival study at McNary Dam, fish released from the tailraces of Wells, Rocky Reach, Rock Island, Wanapum, and Priest Rapids Dams were detected at McNary Dam and at the subsequent downstream arrays. These data were used to generate route-specific survival probabilities using single-release models from fish released in the Mid-Columbia River.

We document trends in passage and survival probabilities at McNary Dam for yearling Chinook and sockeye salmon and juvenile steelhead released during studies in the Mid-Columbia River. Trends in the survival and passage of these juvenile salmonid species are presented and discussed. However, comparisons made across years and between study groups are not possible because of differences in the source of the test fish, the type of acoustic tags used, the absence of the use of passive integrated transponder tags in some of the release groups, differences in tagging and release protocols, annual differences in dam operations and configurations, differences in how the survival models were constructed (that is, number of routes that could be estimated given the number of fish detected), and the number and length of reaches included in the analysis (downstream reach length and arrays). Despite these differences, the data we present offer a unique opportunity to examine the migration behavior and survival of a group of fish that otherwise would not be studied. This is particularly true for sockeye salmon because little information is available about their survival as they pass hydroelectric dams in the lower Columbia River.

Collecting information on fish released in the Mid-Columbia River, as well as on fish released 8 kilometers upstream of McNary Dam, allowed us to evaluate similarities and differences in passage and survival probabilities. In general, juvenile salmonids released in the Mid-Columbia River and detected at and downstream of McNary Dam showed trends in passage and survival probabilities that were similar to fish released 8 kilometers upstream of McNary Dam. This suggests that increased migration time or length of migration had little effect on behavior and survival of Mid-Columbia River released juvenile salmonids detected at McNary Dam.

Introduction

Hydroelectric projects on the Snake and Columbia Rivers are major sources of mortality for migrating juvenile fish. Impoundments caused by dams indirectly may contribute to mortality by slowing the migration of juvenile salmonids (Raymond, 1968, 1979; Plumb and others, 2006), thus increasing exposure to predators and disease in reservoirs. Passage through dams is a direct source of mortality (Mesa, 1994; Whitney and others, 1997) and is cumulative for populations negotiating multiple dams. Few studies have been conducted using acoustic telemetry techniques encompassing long reaches and passage through multiple hydroelectric projects. This technology makes it possible to collect detailed information at dams as well as survival in reaches throughout the Columbia River.

In the spring of 2006, the U. S. Geological Survey (USGS) applied acoustic telemetry technology at McNary Dam to obtain approach, passage, and survival information for yearling Chinook salmon and juvenile steelhead (Adams and others, 2008). Results from that study indicated that higher spill discharge generally results in higher fish passage through the spillway and, consequently, higher fish survival through the entire dam. In addition, the combination of detailed three-dimensional (3-D) approach paths of fish and high passage effectiveness estimated for the south spill bays aided in the design and location of surface bypass structures installed for the migration study period in 2007.

The USGS conducted behavioral and survival studies during 2007, 2008, and 2009, at McNary Dam to assess the performance of the new temporary spillway weirs (TSWs) during various spill operations. In 2007, a "2006 Modified spill" and "2007 Test spill" were planned for evaluation of TSW performance. During the spring of 2007, however, the USGS observed few differences in spill operations between the two spill treatments. Consequently, no measurable differences in fish passage and survival were observed between the spill treatments. Spill treatments were not planned in spring 2008 or 2009; however, in 2008, two distinct flow conditions were evident. The flow conditions were characterized by 40 percent of project discharge spilled during the first half of the spring season and 60 percent of project discharge spilled during the second half of the spring season. Results indicated that more yearling Chinook salmon and juvenile steelhead passed through the TSWs during 40 percent spill than during 60 percent spill. However, spillway survival and survival through all routes for both species were slightly higher during 60 percent spill than during 40 percent spill. Fish passage efficiency (FPE) for yearling Chinook salmon was higher during 60 percent spill than during 40 percent spill.

In addition to the acoustic-tagged fish released specifically for studies at McNary Dam, several thousand additional fish migrate past McNary Dam every year that are tagged and released from dams in the Mid-Columbia River by Grant and Chelan County Public Utility Districts (PUDs). Because the tags implanted in Mid-Columbia released fish were compatible with the USGS acoustic receivers at McNary Dam, it also was possible to obtain movement information on Mid-Columbia released fish at McNary Dam. Consequently, a pilot study was conducted on acoustic-tagged fish released from the Mid-Columbia River in 2006 and 2007 to determine the feasibility of estimating passage and survival for these fish as they migrate past McNary Dam. Hardiman and others (2009) demonstrated that passage and survival through McNary Dam of juvenile salmonids released in the Mid-Columbia River could be assessed. Hardiman and others (2009) concluded that trends in passage and survival of Mid-Columbia River released juvenile salmonids were similar to fish released 8 km upstream of McNary Dam; suggesting that increased migration time or migration distance had little effect on behavior and survival of Mid-Columbia River released juvenile salmonids at McNary Dam.

Using the detection systems in place for studies at McNary Dam and tagged fish released in the Mid-Columbia River as part of other studies is a cost-effective way to obtain passage and survival information specific to fish migrating from the Mid-Columbia River. Grant and Chelan County PUDs tagged and released yearling Chinook salmon, juvenile sockeye salmon, and juvenile steelhead in the Mid-Columbia River during 2008 and 2009. A subset of fish also was implanted with passive integrated transponder (PIT) tags that allowed these fish to be monitored in the bypass system at McNary Dam. The PIT tags were used to determine if the fish passed through the turbines or the bypass system.

Description of Study Area

McNary Dam is the fourth dam upstream of the mouth of the Columbia River, located 470 river kilometers (rkm) upstream of the Pacific Ocean and 52 rkm downstream of the confluence of the Columbia and Snake Rivers. The reservoir formed by McNary Dam (Lake Wallula) extends 98 rkm upstream to the Hanford Reach on the Columbia River, and impounds 16 rkm of the Snake River upstream to Ice Harbor Dam. The river downstream of McNary Dam (Lake Umatilla) is impounded by John Day Dam located 123 rkm downstream of McNary Dam. The study area encompassed 482 km, extending from the tailrace of Wells Dam (rkm 830), the upper most release point for tagged fish, to our most downstream detection array located at John Day Dam (rkm 348; fig. 1).

McNary Dam is oriented perpendicular to the river channel with a navigation lock, spillway, powerhouse, and earthen dam. The spillway is 399 m long with 22 vertical lift-type spill gates that regulate discharge through the dam. The spillway discharges water at the ogee crest approximately 14 m below the water surface. The powerhouse at McNary Dam is 433 m long with 14 turbine units. Each turbine unit has a generating capacity of 70 megawatts and a hydraulic capacity of 16.6 thousand ft³/s. The turbine intakes are about 19 m deep and are divided into three fully isolated slots. Each slot has a vertical barrier screen, trash rack (designed to prevent large debris from entering the turbines), and an extended-length submersible barrier screen that guides downstream migrating fish away from the turbine intakes and into a fish collection channel. Guided fish are then routed through a series of pipes and channels to a juvenile fish bypass facility and held in concrete raceways where the fish await downstream transportation by barge or truck, or are routed back into the river to continue their migration. No study fish with PIT tags were barged during the spring study periods in 2008 and 2009.

Two TSW designs were tested during 2008 and 2009. TSW design 1 was installed in spill bay 19 during 2008 and spill bay 4 during 2009. TSW design 2 was installed in spill bay 20 during 2008 and 2009. Each TSW was comprised of a weir crest, set atop the spill leaf gate in the spill bay. The weir crest extended from the top of the ogee crest to about 2.4 m below the surface, thereby causing water to spill from the surface of the forebay rather than from 14 m below the surface like conventional spill bays. Discharge over the TSWs was a function of forebay elevation, and because TSW design 1 was about 0.2 m deeper than TSW design 2, discharge through TSW design 1 was, on average, slightly greater (about 600 ft³/s) than discharge through TSW design 2. The difference in the elevation of the TSWs was the result of structural differences to test the efficacy of varying entrance conditions for passing juvenile salmonids.

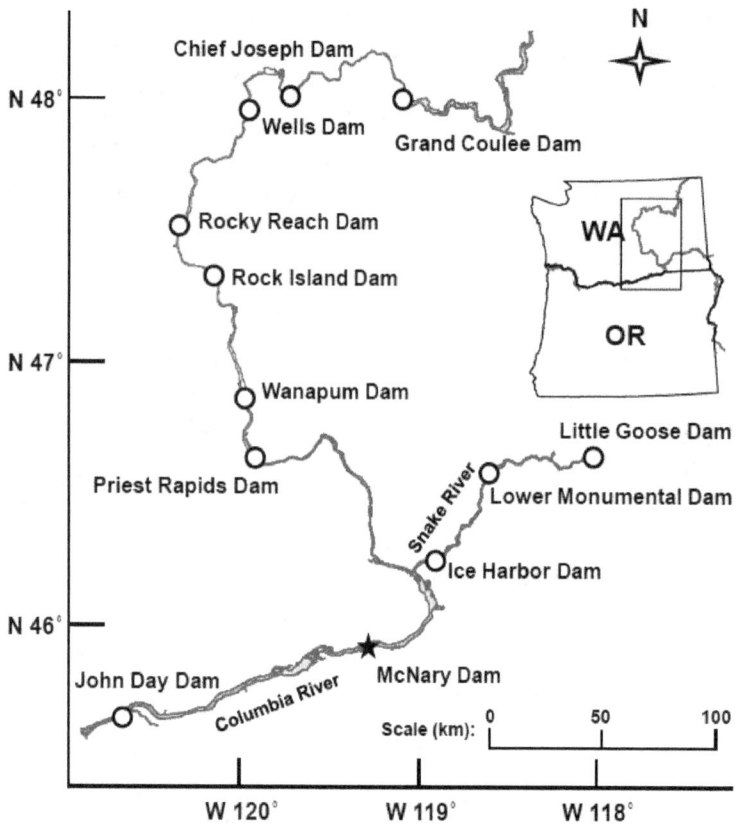

Figure 1. Map showing location of McNary Dam relative to other major hydroelectric projects on the Columbia and Snake Rivers.

Methods

Acoustic Telemetry System

The acoustic telemetry system consisted of acoustic receivers, hydrophones, and transmitters. A total of 94 hydrophones (model 590; Hydroacoustic Technology, Inc., HTI; Seattle, WA) were deployed throughout the 132 km study area in 2008. Each hydrophone had a 290° beam width and was continuously monitored by one of five acoustic tag receivers (ATR; model 290; HTI) in the McNary Dam forebay, or 1 of 20 remote acoustic tag data loggers (ATDL; model 295-X; HTI) upstream and downstream of McNary Dam. In 2009, 113 hydrophones were deployed throughout the 102-km study area and each 290° hydrophone was continuously monitored by 1 of 7 ATRs or 1 of 17 ATDLs.

During 2008 and 2009, the acoustic telemetry system was designed to collect two-dimensional (2-D) and three-dimensional (3-D) position estimates for the USGS behavioral and survival study. For the analysis of the Mid-Columbia released fish and their survival at McNary Dam, all telemetry arrays were used but 3-D position estimates were not obtained.

Forebay and Dam Hydrophone Arrays

During 2008, 5 hydrophone arrays consisting of 77 hydrophones were linked to 5 ATRs and 3 ATDLs in the forebay of McNary Dam. During 2009, 8 hydrophone arrays consisting of 94 hydrophones linked to 7 ATRs and 3 ATDLs were deployed in the forebay of McNary Dam. Hydrophones were mounted near the surface (less than 2 m below the surface) and near the bottom (greater than 18.3 m below the surface) of the river. Double hydrophone arrays were installed at all dam passage routes to permit the estimation of route-specific detection probabilities and use of the route-specific survival model (RSSM; Skalski and others, 2002). Adams and Liedtke (2009, 2010) provide a detailed description of hydrophone arrays.

Remote Hydrophone Arrays

During 2008, seven remote hydrophone arrays were deployed upstream and downstream of McNary Dam to facilitate estimates of travel time and survival in the 132-km study area. Each array consisted of two or three ATDLs, each connected to a single hydrophone. One array was deployed upstream of McNary Dam in Lake Wallula and six arrays were deployed in Lake Umatilla downstream of McNary Dam. When feasible, hydrophones were deployed on floating barges or pre-existing structures (for example, bridge pilings, navigation markers, and navigation walls) at depths of 1.5–2.1 m, depending on the location. When it was not feasible to mount hydrophones on existing structures, the hydrophones were deployed on steel towers at depths of 4–16 m below the surface of the water. Satellite modems (model iNFINITI® 3100, iDirect, Herndon, VA) were deployed at each array to establish a wireless network between each receiver and data-processing servers at the Columbia River Research Laboratory. This network allowed automated transfer of data, as well as the ability to access and control receivers remotely. All ATDLs and satellite modems were powered by solar-charged batteries.

During 2009, five remote hydrophone arrays were deployed upstream and downstream of McNary Dam. Four of the five arrays consisted of three or four ATDLs, each connected to a single hydrophone. The other array consisted of an ATR connected to five hydrophones. One array was deployed 1 mi upstream of McNary Dam in Lake Wallula and the other four arrays were deployed in Lake Umatilla downstream of McNary Dam. Hydrophones in the array upstream of McNary Dam were deployed on floating barges at a depth of 1.8 m. Hydrophones in the arrays downstream of McNary Dam were deployed about 1 m above the river bottom using steel towers. Cellular modems were deployed at each array to establish a wireless network between each ATDL or ATR and our data processing servers at the Columbia River Research Laboratory. This network allowed automated transfer of data, as well as the ability to access and control each ATDL and ATR remotely. All ATDLs were powered by solar-charged batteries.

Acoustic Transmitters

Five models of acoustic tags manufactured by HTI were used during the study (table 1). Juvenile steelhead and yearling Chinook salmon were implanted with Model 795E or 795E/PIT tags in 2008 and Model 795E/PIT or 795LE tags in 2009. Model 795E/PIT tags consisted of a model 795E tag mated with a Biomark RFID model TXP148511B PIT tag (8.5×2.12 mm, 0.067 g in air) during the tag building process. Sockeye salmon were implanted with Model 795m acoustic tags in 2008 and Model 795Lm acoustic tags in 2009. All tags broadcast at a frequency of 307 kHz and the pulse width was 1.0 ms. Individual transmitters were assigned a pulse rate ranging between 2,004 and 6,897 ms, providing a unique identifier that enabled the user to distinguish an individual tag from the many thousands of other tags in the river. A complete description of tag settings for each fish release group can be found in Sullivan and others (2008), Steig and others (2009, 2010), and Timko and others (2010). Tag-life studies conducted by Chelan County PUD (CPUD) in 2008 and CPUD and Grant County PUD (GPUD) in 2009 indicated the average tag life for tags implanted in juvenile steelhead and Chinook salmon was between 19.0 and 25.8 days, depending on tag model and year (table 1). The average tag life, based on tag-life studies, for tags implanted in sockeye salmon was between 17.0 and 21.5 days, depending on tag model and year.

Table 1. Specifications for HTI acoustic transmitters surgically implanted in Mid-Columbia River released juvenile steelhead and yearling Chinook and sockeye salmon, 2008–09.

[HTI, Hydroacoustic Technologies Incorporated Species: CH1, yearling Chinook salmon; SOC, sockeye salmon; STH, juvenile steelhead. mm, millimeter; mm³, cubic millimeter; g, grams; d, days]

Species	Model	Diameter (mm)	Length (mm)	Volume (mm³)	Weight (g)	Average tag life (d)
			2008			
SOC	795m	6.8	16.5	599	0.75	17.0
CH1, STH	795E	6.8	21.0	762	1.50	19.0
CH1, STH	795E/PIT	6.8	21.8	791	1.65	25.8
			2009			
SOC	795Lm	5.0	17.5	343	0.65	21.5
CH1, STH	795LE	6.8	18.0	654	1.50	23.0
CH1, STH	795E/PIT	6.8	21.8	791	1.65	25.8

Fish Tagging and Release

The Mid-Columbia River released fish were tagged and released by personnel from HTI, LGL Limited, Chelan County PUD (CPUD), and Grant County PUD (GPUD). The standard methodology and protocols used were based on studies conducted in 1999 and 2000 (Stevenson and others, 2000; Skalski and others, 2001). The source, collection, and release sites for each species and release group are briefly documented in this report (see also appendix A). For a detailed description of collection, transport, and tagging procedures, see Sullivan and others (2008), Steig and others (2009, 2010), and Timko and others (2010). Juvenile salmonids were collected from the Rocky Reach juvenile surface collector and gatewell dipping from Wanapum Dam in 2008 and 2009, and additionally from gatewell dipping from Priest Rapids Dam in 2009 (table 2). For all Mid-Columbia experimental groups, handling protocols (that is, collection, transport, tagging, holding, and release) were standardized as much as possible among release groups to reduce the potential for bias (Stevenson and others, 2000; Skalski and others, 2001). All acoustic transmitters were surgically implanted. Fish were held 24–48 h before tagging, and again for 24–48 h after tagging, to allow for adequate recovery.

Table 2. Summary of species, collection sources, release dates, fish per release, and release sites for acoustic-tagged juvenile salmonids released in the Mid-Columbia River by Chelan and Grant County PUDs during 2008–09.

[Collection source: PG, Priest Rapids Dam Gatewells; RC, Rocky Reach Collector; WG, Wanapum Dam Gatewells. Release site: PG, Priest Rapids Dam; RC, Rocky Reach Collector; RI, Rock Island Dam; RR, Rocky Reach Dam; WA, Wanapum Dam; WE, Wells Dam; VB, Vantage Bridge]

Species	Collection source	Release dates	Fish per release	Release site
Chinook	WG	May 8–June 5, 2008	30–80	VB
Chinook	RC	April 24–May 30, 2008	21–27	RR
Steelhead	WG	May 8–June 3, 2008	8–26	PR, RI, WA
Steelhead	RC	April 24–June 1, 2008	23–27	RR
Sockeye	RC	May 13–June 6, 2008	6–24	RI, RR, WE
Chinook	RC	April 25–May 11, 2009	19–29	RR
Steelhead	PG,WG	May 2–May 25, 2009	20–53	PR, RI, WA
Steelhead	RC	April 27–May 11, 2009	19–32	RR
Sockeye	PG,WG	May 14–June 1, 2009	30–52	PR, RI, WA
Sockeye	RC	May 15–June 8, 2009	29–41	RC, RR, WE

Tagging and release procedures were similar to those used by the USGS in the lower Columbia and Snake Rivers, although differences were observed. Releases were made from a helicopter (Mid-Columbia releases only) or from a boat. One notable difference from USGS procedures was that CPUD Mid-Columbia River released fish were held for up to 48 h after tagging to allow for recovery from the tagging procedures, to remove any post-tagging mortalities, and to identify any early acoustic tag failure (GPUD-released fish were held 24 h post-tagging). The procedures for USGS released fish were to hold fish for 18–34 h after tagging. The USGS surgically tagged and released yearling Chinook salmon and juvenile steelhead from Hat Rock State Park to assess survival at McNary Dam from April 18 to June 3, 2008, and from April 17 to June 2, 2009. Adams and Liedtke (2009, 2010) provide a detailed description of tagging and release procedures for USGS released fish.

Data Analyses

Signal Processing and Verification

Passage routes, approach distributions, and travel times were determined from acoustic transmitter signals collected by hydrophones at the dam and in the reservoir. First, valid acoustic signals were separated from ambient noise using the HTI software MarkTags©. Files were compiled and the auto-marking software identified individual tags to be verified by data technicians. Tracking parameters were set in the software to minimize the marking of false detections caused by noise or overlap of individual tags and to maximize detections of available fish (based on a tag list of all possible tags). Tag lists were generated for each batch based on a search duration determined by the estimated travel time information. Once fish records were verified by technicians, a second round of processing occurred with a wider parameter set and search duration and a smaller tag list to look for remaining undetected fish. All verified fish records were then compiled and detections of individual fish were identified and given to data technicians for manual marking of the individual tracks. After manual marking, the MarkTags© software was used to assign a date and time for the beginning and end of each valid acoustic track. The detections were then used to estimate the proximity of an acoustic transmitter to hydrophones and to determine the locations of implanted acoustic transmitters.

Travel Times and Rates

We evaluated travel times and rates of fish in reaches upstream and downstream of McNary Dam. Travel times of juvenile salmonids often are not normally distributed, have a skewed distribution, and are highly variable (Giorgi and others, 1997). Much of this variability arises from the dispersal of fish as they travel downstream after release (Zabel, 1994; Zabel and Anderson, 1997). To account for this, the inverse Gaussian distribution was used to estimate mean travel times and rates and to express the variation about these estimates. For each reach, a mean travel time, mean travel rate, and the mean rate of population spread were estimated by use of the methods described by Zabel and Anderson (1997). The rate of population spread provides an indication of how fast fish disperse as they migrate. The amount of error was expressed by calculating 95-percent confidence intervals about the mean travel rate (Zabel, 1994, 2002; Zabel and Anderson, 1997). Mean travel rates among reaches were selected for comparison as a way to standardize across release sites because mean travel time is dependent on reach length and mean travel rate is not.

Passage Determinations

Passage at McNary Dam was assigned as either powerhouse (includes both turbine and bypass routes), spillway, or TSW (bay-specific). Passage routes were determined using the last two hydrophones an acoustic-tagged fish was closest to that clearly defined a route. An automated program was constructed using SAS® software (SAS Institute Inc., Cary, N.C.) to determine which hydrophone the fish was closest to and which route the fish used to pass through the dam. In some instances, passage could not be determined due to ambient noise that mimicked valid tag signals, faint and/or intermittent fish records, or conflicting information between the primary and secondary pulses from the tags among the detections systems. For these fish, it was necessary to determine passage manually by using the MarkTags© software. If there was not enough information, or conflicting information, these fish were categorized as unknown passage. In addition to the manual determinations, a number of random fish records also were reviewed manually as a quality assurance measure to verify that the passage route assignments made by the SAS® program were correct. Once the final dataset was compiled, a series of data checks were conducted to verify detection records. All last detections were examined for any negative travel times which would indicate the possibility of a false record. Records also were reviewed manually when passage was assigned by proximity if the last two hydrophone detections were more than 2 minutes apart.

Survival Model Specifics

The RSSM (Skalski and others, 2002) was used to estimate passage and survival probabilities. Variation in the estimates also was estimated and reported as 95-percent profile likelihood confidence intervals. The foundation of the RSSM is based on the single release-recapture Cormack-Jolly-Seber models (CJS) (Cormack, 1964; Jolly, 1965; and Seber, 1965) and the paired release-recapture model of Burnham and others (1987). The RSSM partitions survival among reservoir and route-specific components and uses a branching process to estimate conditional route-specific passage probabilities (table 3 and fig. 2). The model also expresses parameters downstream of the dam as a function of each release group. Model fit was assessed by examining residuals of observed versus expected capture history counts (appendix B).

8

Table 3. Definitions of fish detection, passage, and survival parameters at McNary Dam, 2008–09.

[Estimates were obtained using a single release, route-specific survival model and represent the survival probability from detection in front of the route to the first detection array downstream of McNary Dam. Parameter: PH, powerhouse; SP, spillway; TSW temporary spillway weir; PR, unconditional probability; P, detection probability; S, survival probability. Source: MLE, maximum likelihood estimate]

Parameter	Source	Definition
PH	MLE	Unconditional probability of powerhouse passage (turbines and bypass combined).
SP	MLE	Probability of spillway passage, conditional on the fish not passing the powerhouse.
TSW1 [1]	MLE	Probability of TSW design 1 passage, conditional on the fish not passing the powerhouse or spillway.
TSW2 [1]	MLE	Probability of TSW design 2 passage, conditional on the fish not passing the powerhouse or spillway.
PR_{Ph}	Derived	Unconditional probability of powerhouse passage (same as PH above).
PR_{Sp}	Derived	Unconditional probability of spillway passage.
PR_{TSW1} [1]	Derived	Unconditional probability of TSW design 1 passage.
PR_{TSW2} [1]	Derived	Unconditional probability of TSW design 2 passage.
P_{Fb}	MLE	Detection probability of the forebay entrance site.
P_{Ph1}	MLE	Detection probability of first powerhouse array.
P_{Ph2}	MLE	Detection probability of second powerhouse array.
P_{Ph}	Derived	Overall detection probability of the powerhouse.
P_{Sp1}	MLE	Detection probability of first spillway array.
P_{Sp2}	MLE	Detection probability of second spillway array.
P_{Sp}	Derived	Overall detection probability of the spillway.
P_{TSW11} [1]	MLE	Detection probability of first TSW design 1 array.
P_{TSW12} [1]	MLE	Detection probability of second TSW design 1 array.
P_{TSW1} [1]	Derived	Overall detection probability of TSW design 1.
P_{TSW21} [1]	MLE	Detection probability of first TSW design 2 array.
P_{TSW22} [1]	MLE	Detection probability of second TSW design 2 array.
P_{TSW2} [1]	Derived	Overall detection probability of TSW design 2.
P_{TSW} [12]	MLE	Overall detection probability of TSW design 1 and TSW design 2 (estimated from downstream detection arrays under the CJS model).
P_R	MLE	Detection probability of the first detection array downstream of McNary Dam.
λ	MLE	Lambda. Joint probability of surviving and being detected by all detection arrays downstream of the first detection array downstream of McNary Dam.
S_{Pool}	MLE	Pool survival probability. Survival probability from upstream boundary of reservoir to detection at the forebay entrance.
S_{Fb}	MLE	Forebay survival probability. Survival probability from point of detection at forebay entrance to point of detection within a passage route.
S_{All_routes}	Derived	Survival probability through all passage routes. The probability of survival from the upstream boundary of the dam (dam face) to detection at the first downstream detection array; it includes all routes of passage, the tailrace, and section of river to the first downstream detection array. The probability of survival through each route of passage is weighted by the probability of passage through each route (that is, $(S_{Spill} \times P_{Spill})$ + $(S_{Bypass} \times P_{Bypass}) + (S_{Turbine} \times P_{Turbine})$) where "S" is the probability of survival and "P" is the probability of passage. Similar to concrete survival but uses single-release model.
S_{Sp}	MLE	Spillway survival probability.
S_{Ph}	MLE	Powerhouse survival probability.
S_{TSW1} [1]	MLE	TSW design 1 survival probability.
S_{TSW2} [1]	MLE	TSW design 2 survival probability.

[1]Parameter was not estimable in 2006 because TSWs were not present.

[2]Parameter was estimated in 2007 only due to absence of double array at TSWs in 2007.

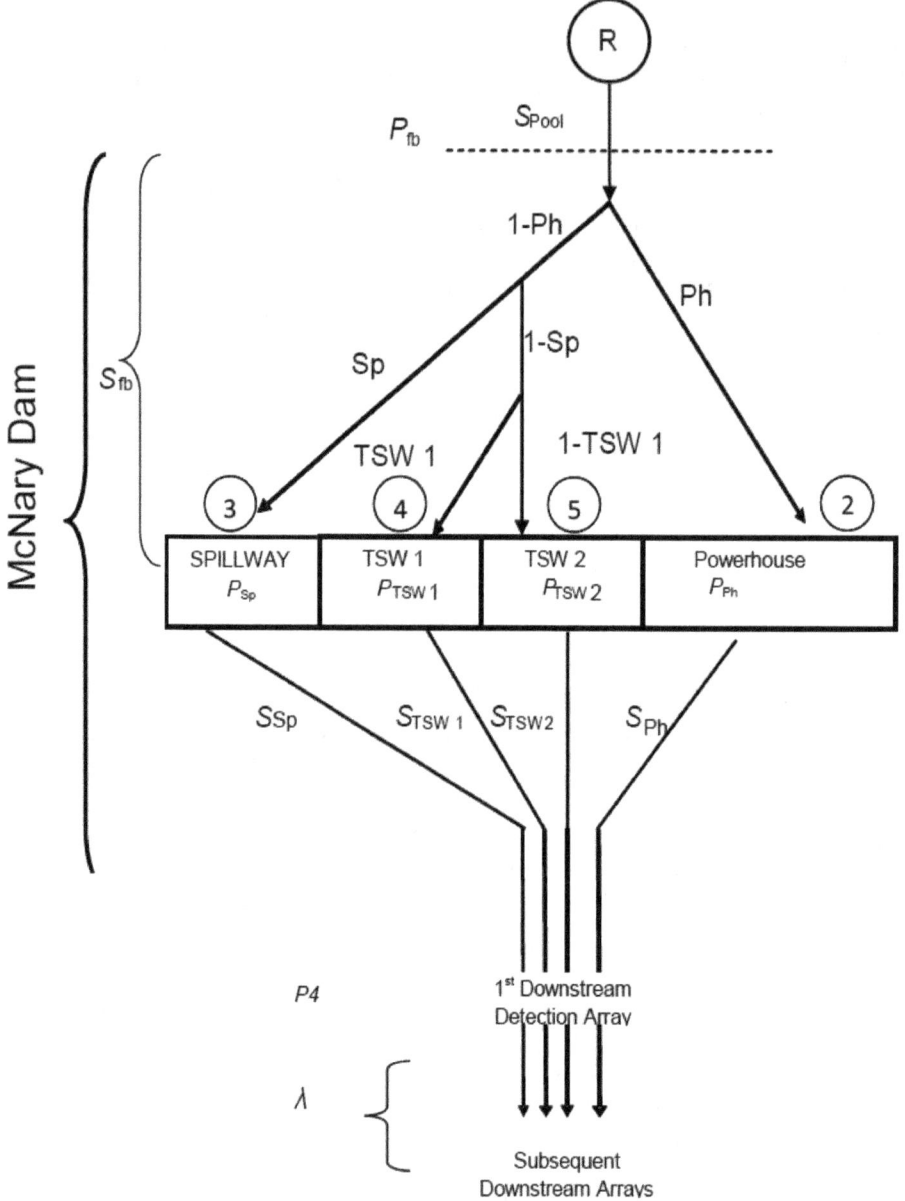

Figure 2. Schematic of a single release, route-specific survival model whereby survival and detection probabilities are separated among available routes and river reaches upstream and downstream of McNary Dam, 2008–09. Release sites in the Mid-Columbia River are represented by R. Circled numbers indicate passage route codes used in detection histories for each fish. Lambda (λ) is the joint probability of surviving and being detected by telemetry arrays downstream of the first detection array downstream of McNary Dam. For subsets of steelhead that were implanted with PIT tags in 2008–09, a route-specific survival model that incorporated five routes was used where the powerhouse was split into bypass and turbine passage routes.

Season-wide passage and survival was estimated with respect to diel periods (that is, day and night) under which the fish had passed the dam. Day and night periods for analysis were defined by when spill operations changed rather than by sunrise and sunset; day was considered 0600 hours to 1759 hours and night was considered 1800 hours to 0559 hours. Fish were assigned to diel periods based on their time of passage at McNary Dam. For the turbines and the spillway, time of passage was assigned to the last detection of fish in the route of passage. For fish going through the juvenile bypass system, passage was assigned using the first detection on the PIT-tag detection coils.

Parameter Estimation

Detection histories for each fish form the basis of mark-recapture models and allow for the estimation of survival and detection probabilities. In general, survival and detection probabilities are estimated by:

1. creating detection histories for each fish;
2. estimating the probability of each possible detection history from the number of fish with that detection history (that is, from the observed frequencies of each detection history); and
3. using maximum likelihood methods to find parameter estimates of survival, passage, and detection probabilities that were most likely, given the observed set of detection histories.

The User Specified Estimation Routine software program (USER 4.4.1) was used to implement the RSSM and estimate passage, survival, and detection parameters (Lady and others, 2009). To prepare the data for input into USER, records for each fish were summarized into detection histories to indicate the route of passage for each fish, whether fish were detected in the first, second, or both detection arrays within each route, and whether fish were detected at arrays downstream of the dam. The RSSM used a primary likelihood to estimate survival and passage probabilities and a secondary likelihood to estimate route-specific detection probabilities. Digit 1 indicated the release; digit 2 indicated detection at the forebay entrance site (1 = detected, 0 = not detected); digit 3 indicated route of passage for each fish, coded by numbers indicating passage route; and digits 4 and 5 indicated detection at subsequent downstream arrays. For example, the detection history 11301 indicates a fish that was released upstream of the dam, was detected at the forebay entrance site, passed through the spillway, was not detected at the first downstream array, but was subsequently detected at a minimum of at least one of the downstream arrays downstream of the first array (subsequent downstream arrays were pooled to estimate λ).

The secondary likelihood was used within-route detection histories to calculate the detection probability of each route. Within-route histories were composed of two digits and indicated whether fish passing that route were detected by the first array (10), the second array (01), or both arrays (11) within each passage route. Estimation of within-route detection probabilities required a redundant double-detection array for each route.

Each unique detection history had a probability of occurrence that can be specified completely in terms of the survival, passage, and detection probabilities. The expected probability of each detection history was estimated from the observed frequencies for fish with that detection history. Given the expected probability of each detection history and its probability function in terms of survival, passage, and detection probabilities, likelihood methods were used to find the combination of probabilities that most likely would occur, given the observed detection histories. The maximum likelihood function was simply the joint probability of all possible detection histories. More details on the maximum likelihood methods for estimating survival and detection probabilities, including estimation of theoretical variances, are reported in Burnham and others (1987), Lebreton and others (1992), and Skalski and others (2001). After estimating model parameters using maximum likelihood methods, additional parameters such as survival probabilities, passage probabilities, and within-route detection probabilities were estimated as functions of model parameters (table 3). Variances are presented as profile likelihood confidence intervals.

Assumptions of Survival Models

Survival and detection probabilities from CJS models are subject to seven assumptions. For CJS models, these assumptions relate to inferences to the population of interest, error in interpreting acoustic signals, and statistical fit of the data to the structure of the model:

1. Tagged individuals are representative of the population of interest. For example, if the target population is yearling Chinook salmon then the sample of tagged fish should be drawn from that population.

2. Survival probabilities of tagged fish are the same as that of untagged fish. For example, the tagging procedures or detection of fish at downstream telemetry arrays should not influence survival or detection probabilities. If the tag negatively affects survival, then single-reach estimates of survival rates will be biased accordingly.

3. All sampling events are instantaneous. That is, sampling should take place over a short distance relative to the distance between telemetry arrays so that the chance of mortality at a telemetry array is minimized. This assumption is necessary to attribute mortality correctly to a specific river reach. This assumption usually is satisfied by the location of telemetry arrays and the downstream migration rates of juvenile salmonids.

4. The fate of each tagged fish is independent of the fate of other tagged fish. In other words, survival or mortality of one fish has no effect on the survival or mortality of the other fish.

5. The prior detection history of a tagged fish has no effect on its subsequent survival. This assumption could be violated if parts of the river are not monitored for tagged fish. For example, for PIT-tagged fish some fish repeatedly may pass through fish bypasses where PIT-tag readers are located, whereas other fish consistently may pass through spillways, which are not monitored. If fish passing through these routes have different survival rates, then this assumption could be violated. For acoustic telemetry, this assumption usually is satisfied by the passive nature of detecting acoustic tags, by monitoring all routes of passage at a dam, and by monitoring the entire cross-section of the river channel.

6. All tagged fish alive at a sampling location have the same detection probability. This assumption could also be violated as described in assumption 5, but usually is satisfied with acoustic telemetry by monitoring the entire cross section of the river channel.

7. All tags are identified correctly and the status of tagged fish (that is, alive or dead) is known without error. The assumption is that fish do not lose their tags and that the tag is functioning when the fish is in the study area. Additionally, the assumption is that all detections are of live fish and that dead fish are not detected and interpreted as live (that is, false-positive detections).

Two additional assumptions that are specific to the RSSM model include:

8. The two detection arrays within each route are independent. This assumption is necessary to obtain valid estimates of route-specific detection probabilities. To fulfill this assumption, fish detected in one array should have the same probability of detection in the second array compared to fish not detected in the first array.

9. Passage routes of acoustic-tagged fish are known without error. This assumption is important in order to avoid bias in passage and survival probabilities.

Tag-life studies were conducted to estimate the probability of tag failure at any point in time after tags were turned on (see appendix C). Because marked fish were released from as far as 358 km upstream of McNary Dam, and 482 km upstream of the detection site farthest downstream of McNary Dam, it was important to determine the probability that tags used to mark fish were still active when fish were passing the detection sites. Significant premature failure of transmitters can negatively bias survival estimates because survival models will interpret tag failure as mortality.

Results

Dam Operations, Environmental Conditions, and Treatment Tests in 2008

Mean total discharge through McNary Dam from April 30 to June 21, 2008, was 320.5 thousand ft³/s with mean daily discharge ranging from 149.8 to 419.1 thousand ft³/s (fig. 3). Of the total water volume discharged at McNary Dam, the powerhouse discharged 49 percent, the spillway discharged 46 percent, and TSW 19 and TSW 20 discharged 5 percent. Spill occurred over the 24-h diel cycle throughout the spring study. There were no treatments in the spring at McNary Dam in 2008; however, two distinct flow conditions were evident (fig. 4). Discharge through the spillway was 40 percent of the total project discharge from April 30 to May 17 (hereinafter referred to as the early period). Discharge through the spillway from May 18 to June 21 (hereinafter referred to as the late period) was considerably higher than the early period, ranging from 47 to 60 percent of total project discharge. During the spring study, mean daily forebay temperatures increased steadily from 9.4 °C on April 30 to 14.9 °C on June 21.

Differences in spill bay-specific and turbine unit-specific discharge were evident between early and late periods (fig. 5). Discharge among spill bays was more variable in the early period than in the late period when all spill bays were discharging at similar rates during day and night.

Dam Operations and Environmental Conditions in 2009

Mean total discharge through McNary Dam from May 2 to June 20, 2009 was 277.3 thousand ft³/s with mean daily discharge ranging from 183.6 to 349.2 thousand ft³/s (fig. 6). The powerhouse discharged an average of 55 percent of the total water volume through the dam, the spillway discharged an average 39 percent, and the TSWs discharged an average 6 percent. Spill occurred over the 24-h diel cycle throughout the study. There were no treatments in the spring at McNary Dam in 2009. Project discharge and traditional spill increased throughout the season, whereas TSW discharge and powerhouse discharge remained fairly consistent. Percent spill was 40 percent through most of the season until the end of May when percent spill increased to 50 percent, then decreased in early June (fig. 7). Mean daily forebay temperatures increased steadily from 8.9 °C on May 2 to 16.6 °C on June 20. Spill bay-specific and turbine unit-specific discharge were similar during day and night, with slightly higher discharge during the day (fig. 8).

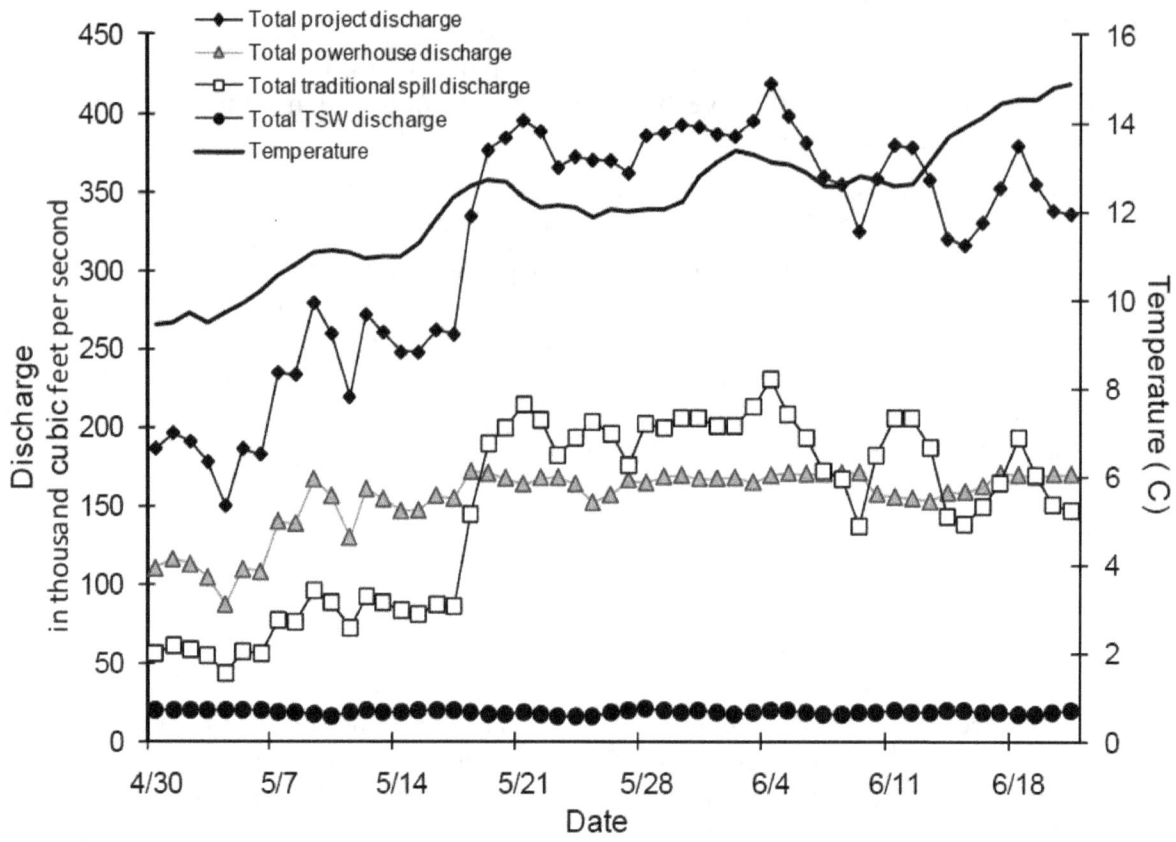

Figure 3. Hydrograph showing mean daily discharge at McNary Dam during spring 2008. Mean daily water temperatures for the forebay of McNary Dam also are shown.

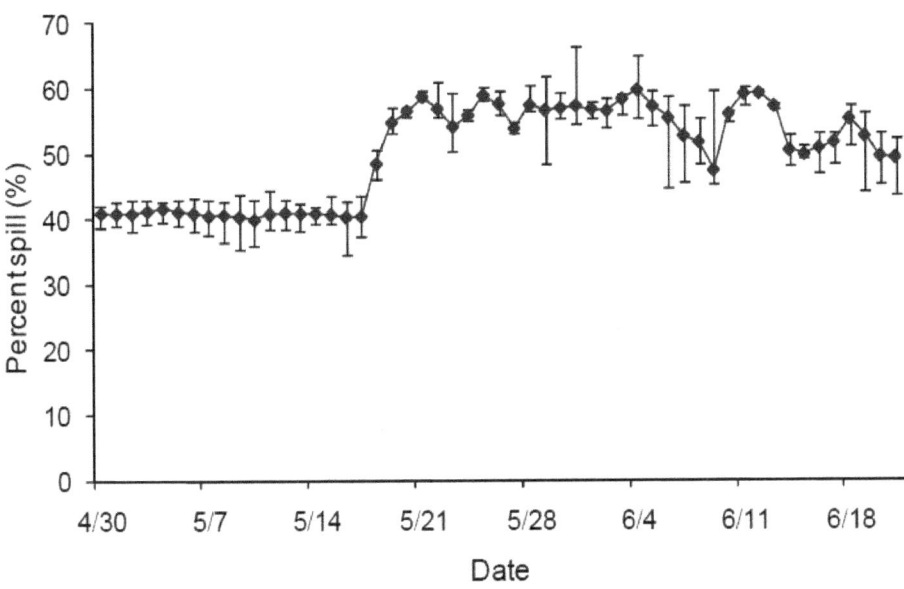

Figure 4. Hydrograph showing mean daily percent spill through McNary Dam, spring 2008. Whiskers represent the minimum and maximum percent spill for each day. The percentage of total discharge spilled includes the water discharged through the temporary spillway weirs.

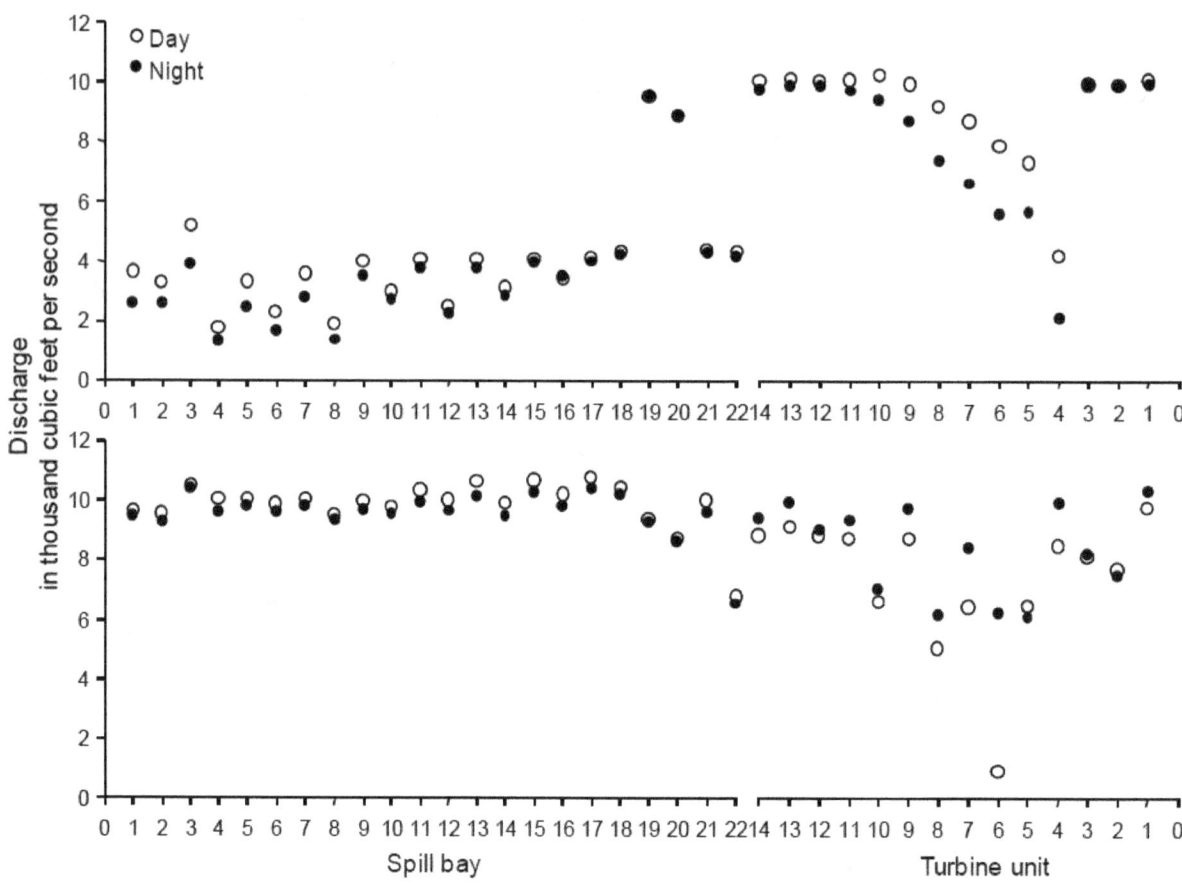

Figure 5. Hydrograph showing mean spill bay-specific and turbine unit-specific discharge (in thousand cubic feet per second) by diel period at McNary Dam, spring 2008, during early (top; April 30 through May 17) and late (bottom; May 18 through June 21) periods. Day is 0600–1759 hours and night is 1800–0559 hours.

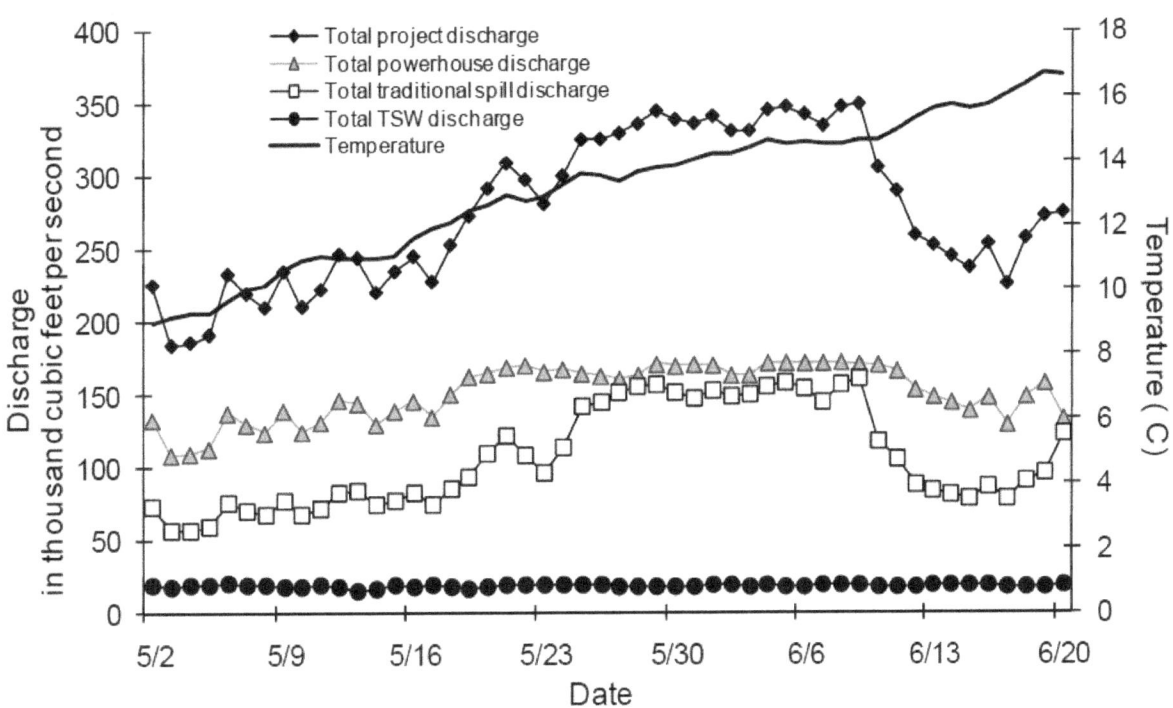

Figure 6. Hydrograph showing mean daily discharge, plotted by date at McNary Dam during spring 2009. Mean daily water temperatures for the forebay of McNary Dam also are shown.

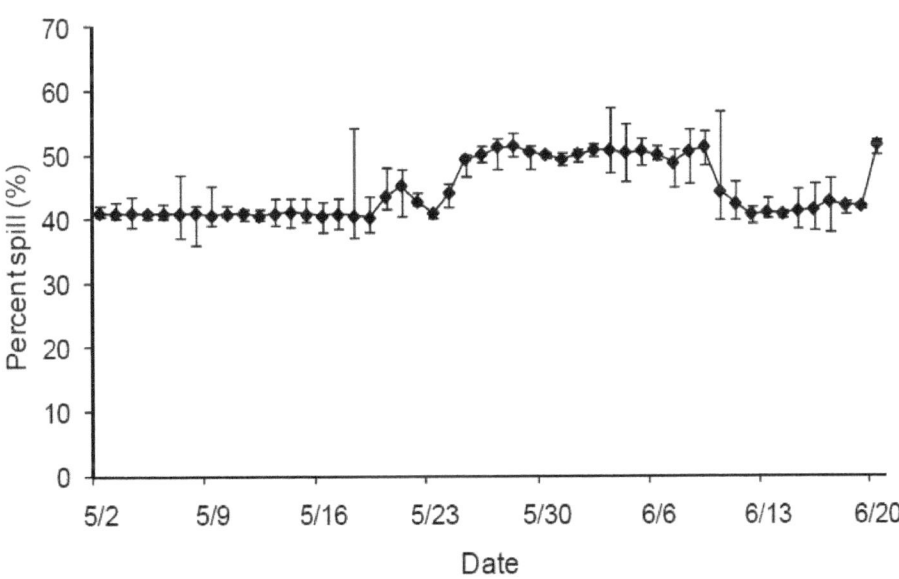

Figure 7. Hydrograph showing mean daily percent spill through McNary Dam during spring 2009. Whiskers represent the minimum and maximum percent spill for each day. The percentage of total discharge spilled includes the water discharged through the temporary spillway weirs.

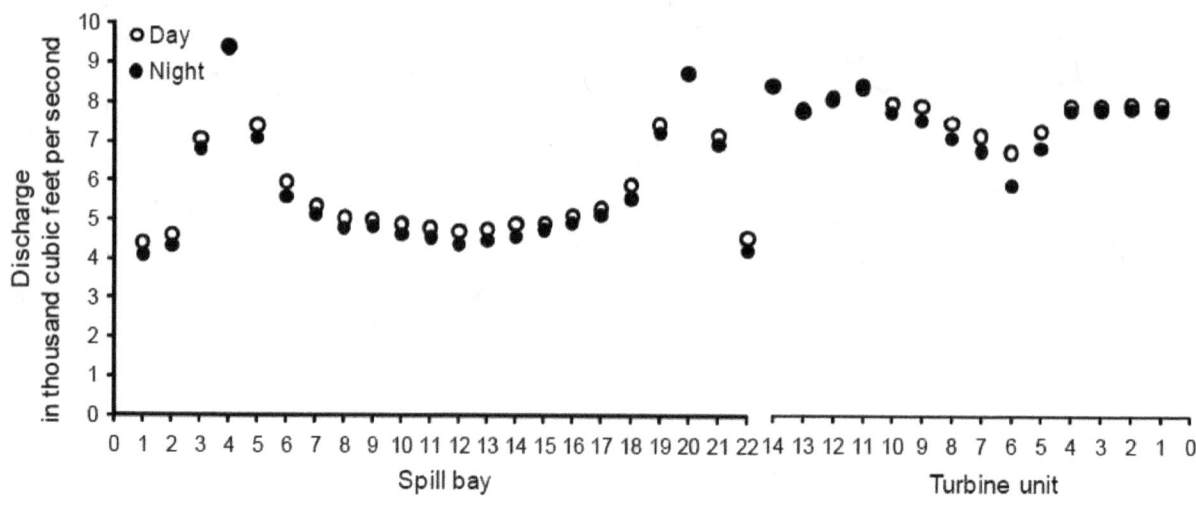

Figure 8. Hydrograph showing mean spill bay-specific and turbine unit-specific discharge by diel period at McNary Dam, May 2 to June 20, 2009. Day is 0600–1759 hours and night is 1800–0559 hours.

Fish Tagging and Release

Juvenile salmonids were tagged and released from the Mid-Columbia River release sites from April 24 to June 6, 2008 and from April 25 to June 8, 2009 (table 4 and appendix A). These release dates overlapped the releases made by the USGS at Hat Rock State Park, Oregon, 10 rkm upstream of McNary Dam, from April 18 to June 4, 2008, and from April 17 to June 2, 2009. Passage dates for Mid-Columbia released fish at McNary Dam encompassed the majority of the population run timing (68–94 percent) for passage dates at McNary Dam according to the Fish Passage Center Smolt Indices for each species (Fish Passage Center, 2010, at *http://www.fpc.org/smolt/historicsmpsubmitdata.html*). Passage date range (minimum and maximum dates of passage), the percent spill observed over passage period, and, consequently, the time period and percent spill associated with passage and survival estimates, are presented for each species in table 5. Survival analyses for Mid-Columbia River released fish in 2008 were conducted on 539 yearling Chinook salmon, 1,888 juvenile steelhead, and 1,084 sockeye salmon that passed McNary Dam. Survival analyses for Mid-Columbia River released fish in 2009 were conducted on 1,860 juvenile steelhead and 3,578 sockeye salmon that passed McNary Dam.

Travel Times and Rates

Average travel times from release to McNary Dam were 2 to 3 days for Priest Rapids Dam, 3 to 4 days for Wanapum Dam, 4 to 7 days for Rock Island Dam, 5 to 9 days for Rocky Reach Dam, and about 6 days for Wells Dam (tables 6 and 7). The mean travel rates ranged from 37.53 to 69.53 km/d in 2008 and from 33.10 to 92.35 km/d in 2009 within the reaches from the Mid-Columbia River release sites to the forebay entrance at McNary Dam (that is, pool) for all species. Travel rates were faster in 2008 than in 2009, for all species and reaches. Within each year, sockeye salmon traveled at the highest rate, followed by juvenile steelhead, and then yearling Chinook salmon. As fish traveled downstream, mean travel rates decreased in the forebay of McNary Dam with average rates ranging from 4.24 to 18.57 km/d in 2008 and from 4.19 to 21.46 km/d in 2009. Travel rates increased in reaches downstream of the dam and were similar to observed travel rates in the reach (that is, pool) upstream of the dam.

Tag-life studies indicated the probability of transmitters being operational when fish reached the detection arrays was relatively high (0.9241 0.9892; appendix C). The mean tag life (15.7 to 26.4 days) for each type of transmitter used in the study exceeded the mean travel times of fish to McNary Dam (2 to 9 days).

Table 4. Summary statistics of fork length and weight for acoustic-tagged juvenile salmonids released in the Mid-Columbia River, 2008–09.

[Release group indicates the agency responsible for the release. CPUD, Chelan County Public Utility District; GPUD, Grant County Public Utility District. Release site: PR, Priest Rapids Dam; RC, Rocky Reach Collector; RR, Rocky Reach Dam; RH, Rock Island Hydro Park; RI, Rock Island Dam; WA, Wanapum Dam; WE, Wells Dam. mm, millimeter; g, grams; Min, minimum; Max, maximum]

Species	Release Group	Release Site	Number of fish	Fork Length (mm)			Weight (g)		
				Mean	Min	Max	Mean	Min	Max
2008									
Chinook	CPUD	RI,RR	949	161	114	224	43	24	119
Steelhead	CPUD	RR	498	187	149	230	58	29	104
Sockeye	CPUD	RC,RH,RR,WE	2,002	117	100	147	16	10	29
Steelhead	GPUD	PR,RI,WA	2,201	186	143	220	59	30	98
2009									
Steelhead	CPUD	RR	175	193	145	228	67	32	121
Sockeye	CPUD	RC,RR,WE	2,031	123	100	158	19	10	49
Steelhead	GPUD	PR, RI,WA	2,096	192	144	220	66	31	90
Sockeye	GPUD	PR, RI,WA	1,943	127	104	210	20	13	86

Table 5. Number of acoustic-tagged juvenile salmonids released in the Mid-Columbia River, number (and percent of those released) that passed McNary Dam, range of passage dates, and corresponding percent spill over dates of passage at McNary Dam, by species, 2008–09.

[Percent spill is the percentage of project discharge spilled and includes the water discharged through the temporary spillway weirs. **Abbreviations**: NA, not applicable]

Species	Period	Number released	Number passed (percent)	Minimum passage date	Maximum passage date	Percent spill
2008						
Chinook	Overall	949	539 (57)	April 30	June 12	51
	Early	NA	182 (19)	April 30	May 17	39
	Late	NA	357 (38)	May 18	June 12	56
Steelhead	Overall	2,699	1,888 (70)	April 30	June 17	51
	Early	NA	412 (15)	April 30	May 17	39
	Late	NA	1,476 (55)	May 18	June 17	55
Sockeye	Overall	2,002	1,084 (54)	May 18	June 21	55
	Early	NA	0 (0)	NA	NA	NA
	Late	NA	1,084 (100)	May 18	June 21	55
2009						
Steelhead	Overall	2,271	1,860 (82)	May 02	June 12	46
Sockeye	Overall	3,974	3,578 (90)	May 18	June 20	47

Table 6. Mean and median travel times, mean travel rates, and the mean rate of population spread by river reach for yearling Chinook salmon, juvenile steelhead, and sockeye salmon released in the Mid-Columbia River during 2008.

[Species: CH1, yearling Chinook salmon; SOC, sockeye salmon; STH, juvenile steelhead. Release site: PR, Priest Rapids Dam; RH, Rock Island Hydro Park; RI, Rock Island Dam; RR, Rocky Reach Dam; WA, Wanapum Dam; WE, Wells Dam. Reach: Reach 1 is defined from release to McNary Dam forebay; Reach 2 is defined from McNary Dam forebay to McNary Dam passage; Reach 3 is defined from McNary Dam passage to first detection array downstream of McNary Dam; Reach 4 is defined from first detection array downstream of McNary Dam to second detection array downstream of McNary Dam. CI, confidence interval; d, day, km, kilometers; km/d, kilometers per day; km^2/d, square kilometers per day. ±, plus or minus; %, percent]

Species	Release site	Reach	Reach length (km)	Number of fish	Mean travel time (d)	Median travel time (d)	Mean travel rate (±95% CI) (km/d)	Mean rate of population spread (±95% CI) (km^2/d)
CH1	RR	1	290	142	7.73	7.03	37.53 (1.96)	32.77 (3.32)
		2	2	134	0.20	0.09	10.01 (2.04)	5.33 (0.55)
		3	24	108	0.75	0.41	31.80 (5.90)	26.75 (3.04)
		4	31	57	0.52	0.54	59.47 (21.01)	56.65 (8.40)
STH	RR	1	290	159	6.03	5.55	48.10 (2.31)	36.09 (3.48)
		2	2	155	0.14	0.08	13.82 (2.12)	5.08 (0.49)
		3	24	116	0.41	0.26	58.23 (7.29)	25.34 (2.80)
		4	31	65	0.47	0.47	66.15 (15.47)	42.40 (5.96)
STH	RI	1	254	353	5.38	4.95	47.23 (1.51)	33.42 (2.25)
		2	2	308	0.36	0.07	5.53 (1.24)	6.64 (0.48)
		3	24	219	0.47	0.26	51.33 (5.36)	27.44 (2.29)
		4	31	133	0.48	0.47	64.96 (11.83)	47.48 (4.94)
STH	WA	1	197.5	233	3.34	3.02	59.05 (2.68)	37.86 (3.08)
		2	2	195	0.13	0.06	15.46 (2.31)	5.86 (0.52)
		3	24	142	0.41	0.27	59.06 (6.12)	23.44 (2.37)
		4	31	85	0.44	0.47	69.95 (16.14)	49.53 (6.24)
STH	PR	1	167	393	2.40	1.99	69.53 (2.59)	40.44 (2.59)
		2	2	344	0.19	0.07	10.78 (1.48)	6.01 (0.41)
		3	24	240	0.40	0.26	60.41 (4.90)	24.22 (1.94)
		4	31	137	0.42	0.45	74.54 (12.67)	48.18 (4.95)
SOC	WE	1	358	134	5.60	5.28	63.92 (3.05)	42.07 (4.36)
		2	2	111	0.38	0.06	5.30 (2.49)	8.09 (0.91)
		3	24	70	0.54	0.53	44.25 (6.90)	21.15 (2.88)
		4	31	59	0.82	0.10	37.89 (25.14)	86.51 (12.65)
SOC	RR	1	290	314	4.48	4.12	64.75 (1.96)	37.33 (2.65)
		2	2	234	0.40	0.05	5.02 (1.64)	8.04 (0.65)
		3	24	177	0.64	0.55	37.41 (4.65)	25.02 (2.30)
		4	31	164	0.24	0.09	129.07 (22.30)	70.65 (6.71)
SOC	RH	1	280	95	4.25	4.04	65.90 (3.36)	33.87 (4.07)
		2	2	78	0.47	0.06	4.24 (2.65)	8.01 (1.05)
		3	24	62	0.85	0.54	28.33 (8.41)	30.23 (4.33)
		4	31	48	0.26	0.09	121.53 (40.84)	70.30 (11.16)
SOC	RI	1	254	187	3.91	3.57	65.01 (2.69)	36.82 (3.30)
		2	2	143	0.29	0.06	6.79 (2.36)	7.73 (0.78)
		3	24	120	0.57	0.53	41.79 (5.91)	24.67 (2.68)
		4	31	100	0.25	0.10	125.53 (27.57)	68.71 (8.08)

Table 7. Mean and median travel times, mean travel rates, and the mean rate of population spread by river reach for juvenile steelhead and sockeye salmon released in the Mid-Columbia River during 2009.

[Species: SOC, sockeye salmon; STH, juvenile steelhead. Release site: PR, Priest Rapids Dam; RI, Rock Island Dam; RR, Rocky Reach Dam; WA, Wanapum Dam; WE, Wells Dam. Reach: Reach 1 is defined from release to McNary Dam forebay; Reach 2 is defined from McNary Dam forebay to McNary Dam passage; Reach 3 is defined from McNary Dam passage to first detection array downstream of McNary Dam; Reach 4 is defined from first detection array downstream of McNary Dam to second detection array downstream of McNary Dam. CI, confidence interval; d, day, km, kilometers; km/d, kilometers per day; km^2/d, square kilometers per day. ±, plus or minus; %, percent]

Species	Release site	Reach	Reach length (km)	Number of fish	Mean travel time (d)	Median travel time (d)	Mean travel rate (±95% CI) (km/d)	Mean rate of population spread (±95% CI) (km^2/d)
STH	RR	1	290	64	8.76	7.93	33.10 (2.23)	26.24 (3.71)
		2	2	64	0.33	0.21	6.03 (1.59)	3.63 (0.51)
		3	22	71	0.56	0.26	39.63 (9.33)	29.16 (3.95)
		4	27	65	0.55	0.55	49.16 (2.88)	8.55 (1.20)
STH	RI	1	254	367	7.53	6.97	33.75 (0.96)	25.51 (1.69)
		2	2	352	0.41	0.19	4.83 (0.76)	4.66 (0.31)
		3	22	488	0.28	0.23	78.83 (3.17)	18.80 (1.09)
		4	27	463	0.53	0.47	51.15 (1.63)	12.98 (0.77)
STH	WA	1	198	266	4.31	3.98	45.82 (1.57)	26.89 (2.06)
		2	2	256	0.48	0.25	4.19 (0.75)	4.22 (0.33)
		3	22	337	0.32	0.24	69.78 (4.24)	22.16 (1.53)
		4	27	323	0.50	0.47	54.19 (1.49)	9.59 (0.67)
STH	PR	1	167	645	3.24	2.67	51.53 (1.57)	36.56 (1.87)
		2	2	620	0.44	0.21	4.59 (0.54)	4.55 (0.24)
		3	22	786	0.27	0.24	82.39 (2.13)	15.69 (0.73)
		4	27	765	0.51	0.47	52.98 (1.13)	11.32 (0.53)
SOC	WE	1	358	304	5.97	5.73	59.95 (1.33)	28.81 (2.08)
		2	2	270	0.10	0.07	19.80 (1.99)	5.27 (0.40)
		3	22	321	0.26	0.18	84.65 (5.54)	25.70 (1.81)
		4	27	325	0.43	0.41	62.71 (1.72)	10.31 (0.72)
SOC	RR	1	290	585	4.88	4.68	59.43 (1.17)	31.80 (1.70)
		2	2	517	0.10	0.06	19.88 (1.59)	5.82 (0.33)
		3	22	629	0.30	0.19	74.42 (4.06)	28.20 (1.46)
		4	27	618	0.45	0.43	59.84 (1.28)	10.84 (0.56)
SOC	RI	1	254	609	4.75	4.46	53.44 (1.12)	30.58 (1.60)
		2	2	565	0.09	0.06	21.46 (1.49)	5.50 (0.30)
		3	22	718	0.30	0.19	72.64 (3.58)	26.86 (1.30)
		4	27	702	0.44	0.42	61.77 (1.14)	10.19 (0.50)
SOC	WA	1	198	433	2.83	2.70	69.68 (1.64)	29.16 (1.79)
		2	2	423	0.13	0.06	14.86 (1.71)	6.56 (0.41)
		3	22	520	0.29	0.20	75.03 (4.11)	25.78 (1.45)
		4	27	516	0.45	0.42	60.41 (1.44)	11.15 (0.63)
SOC	PR	1	167	945	1.81	1.81	92.35 (0.97)	20.35 (0.87)
		2	2	915	0.12	0.06	16.05 (1.09)	5.95 (0.26)
		3	22	1,105	0.31	0.20	71.65 (2.78)	26.12 (1.03)
		4	27	1,090	0.45	0.41	60.45 (1.01)	11.40 (0.45)

Passage Distribution Relative to Diel Period

Mid-Columbia River released fish passed McNary Dam during all hours of the day (figs. 9 and 10). In 2008, 52–54 percent of all species passed during the day (0600–1759) and 46–48 percent passed during the night. Passage was slightly higher for all species during afternoon and evening hours (1400–2100) than during the morning. In 2009, 46 percent of juvenile steelhead and 54 percent of sockeye salmon passed during the day (0600–1759) and the remainder passed during the night. Passage of both juvenile steelhead and sockeye salmon gradually increased over the 24-hour period, peaking between 2100 and 2300 hours for juvenile steelhead, and at 2000 hours for sockeye salmon.

Survival Analyses

Passage and Survival Probabilities in 2008

Route-specific passage and survival probabilities were generated for the Mid-Columbia River released juvenile salmonids passing McNary Dam during spring 2008 (tables 8–11 and figs. 11 and 12). For yearling Chinook salmon, the spillway was the passage route with the highest passage probability overall (0.651), as well as during the late period when a higher proportion of discharge was spilled (0.765; table 8 and fig. 11). In comparison, during the low spill levels of the early period, the probability of passing through the spillway (0.406) was much reduced and most fish passed through the powerhouse (0.441). Although the probability of passage through each TSW during the early period was only 0.076, this was 2–3 times their efficiency during the high spill levels of late period (table 8). Forebay survival for Mid-Columbia released yearling Chinook salmon was 0.984. Survival probabilities for yearling Chinook salmon were highest at the spillway (0.982), followed by TSW 19 (0.951), the powerhouse (0.849), and TSW 20 (0.781; table 8 and fig. 12). Similar patterns in survival probabilities among passage routes were exhibited during early and late periods and wide confidence intervals indicated that there was little difference in survival between the two seasons. However, differences in point estimates of TSW 19 and spillway survival were greater than 10 percent between the two periods.

The overall passage pattern for steelhead released in the Mid-Columbia River was similar to the overall passage pattern for yearling Chinook salmon, with the highest passage probability being the spillway (0.617), followed by the powerhouse (0.184), TSW 20 (0.110), and TSW 19 (0.089). However, unlike Chinook salmon which shifted their passage to the powerhouse during the low spill of the early period, steelhead passage increased through the TSWs during lower spill levels. The route with the second highest probability of passage during the early period for steelhead was TSW 20 (0.239; table 9 and fig. 11). Similar to yearling Chinook salmon, spillway passage probability for juvenile steelhead nearly doubled during the late period, when percent spill increased. Survival in the forebay for the Mid-Columbia River released juvenile steelhead was 0.996. The passage route with the highest survival was the spillway (0.968), followed by TSW 19 (0.921), TSW 20 (0.909), and the powerhouse (0.857). A similar pattern was seen for both early and late periods, but because of high variance associated with survival estimates, we could not distinguish any difference in survival among routes between seasons. Furthermore, differences in point estimates of survival between early and late periods were small (less than 0.040) except for the difference in survival through TSW 19, which was 0.081.

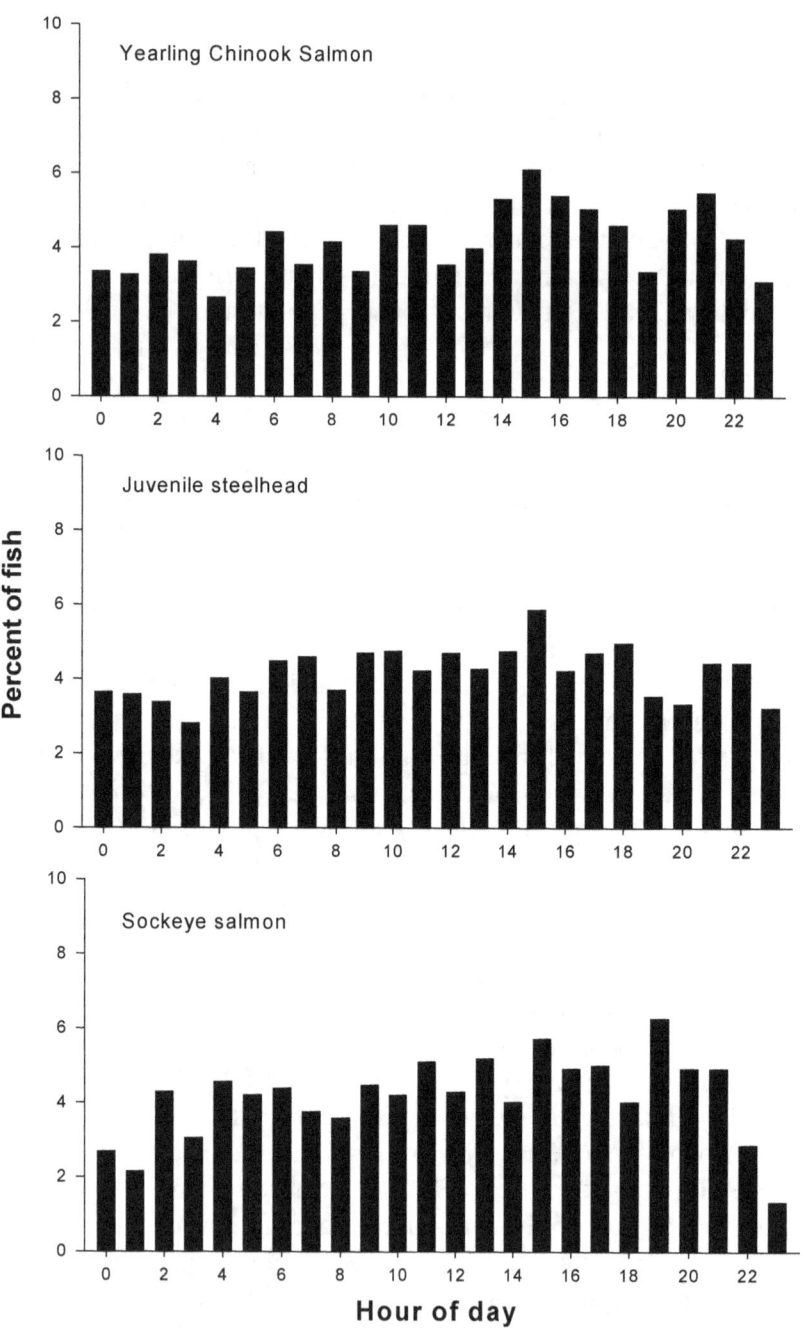

Figure 9. Graphs showing frequency distribution of the last detection hour (usually passage time) at McNary Dam for Mid-Columbia River released yearling Chinook and sockeye salmon and juvenile steelhead during 2008.

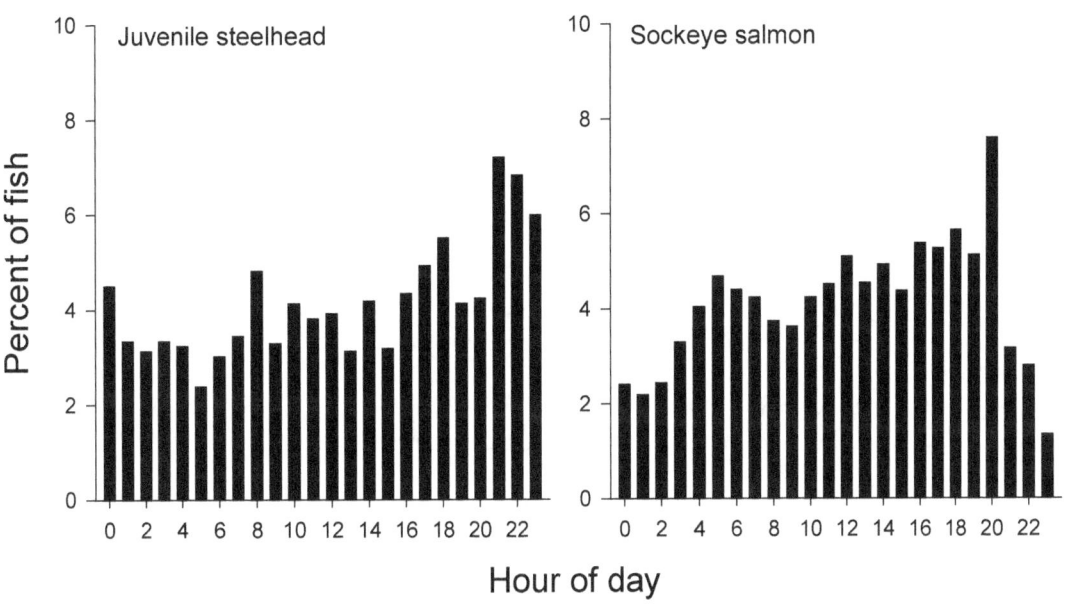

Figure 10. Graphs showing frequency distribution of the last detection hour (usually passage time) at McNary Dam for Mid-Columbia River released juvenile steelhead and sockeye salmon during 2009.

Table 8. Route-specific passage (*N*=539) and survival (single-release) probabilities for yearling Chinook salmon implanted with an acoustic tag, presented by early period (40 percent spill), late period (60 percent spill), and overall, spring 2008.

[The early period was from April 30 to May 17, 2008, and late period was from May 18 to June 12, 2008. Single-release estimates represent survival from passage at McNary Dam to Big Blalock Island located 24 kilometers downstream of McNary Dam. Fish were released at Rock Island and Rocky Reach Dams. LCL, lower confidence limit; UCL, upper confidence limit]

Estimate (location)	Early period (LCL,UCL)	Late period (LCL,UCL)	Overall (LCL,UCL)
	Passage probabilities		
Powerhouse	0.441 (0.370,0.514)	0.174 (0.138,0.214)	0.259 (0.224,0.296)
TSW 20	0.076 (0.044,0.121)	0.036 (0.020,0.057)	0.049 (0.033,0.068)
TSW 19	0.076 (0.044,0.121)	0.025 (0.013,0.044)	0.042 (0.027,0.060)
Spillway	0.406 (0.336,0.478)	0.765 (0.721,0.805)	0.651 (0.611,0.689)
	Single-release survival probabilities		
Forebay	NA	NA	0.984 (0.964,0.997)
Powerhouse	0.868 (0.758,0.968)	0.828 (0.701,0.942)	0.849 (0.767,0.926)
TSW 20	0.775 (0.493,0.986)	0.788 (0.502,1.003)	0.781 (0.582,0.943)
TSW 19	[1]1.000	0.883 (0.551,1.078)	[2]0.951 (0.793,1.034)
Spillway	0.894 (0.783,0.994)	1.004 (0.945,1.072)	0.982 (0.930,1.040)
All routes	[2]0.881 (0.809,0.956)	0.962 (0.906,1.029)	[2]0.937 (0.892,0.987)

[1]Survival probability and confidence limits were not estimable using maximum likelihood methods because we detected 100 percent (14/14) of the fish passing this route at downstream detection arrays. Although the modeling software could not produce an estimate, our best estimate of survival is 100 percent.
[2]Variance from parameter in footnote 1 not accounted for in other estimates derived from this parameter.

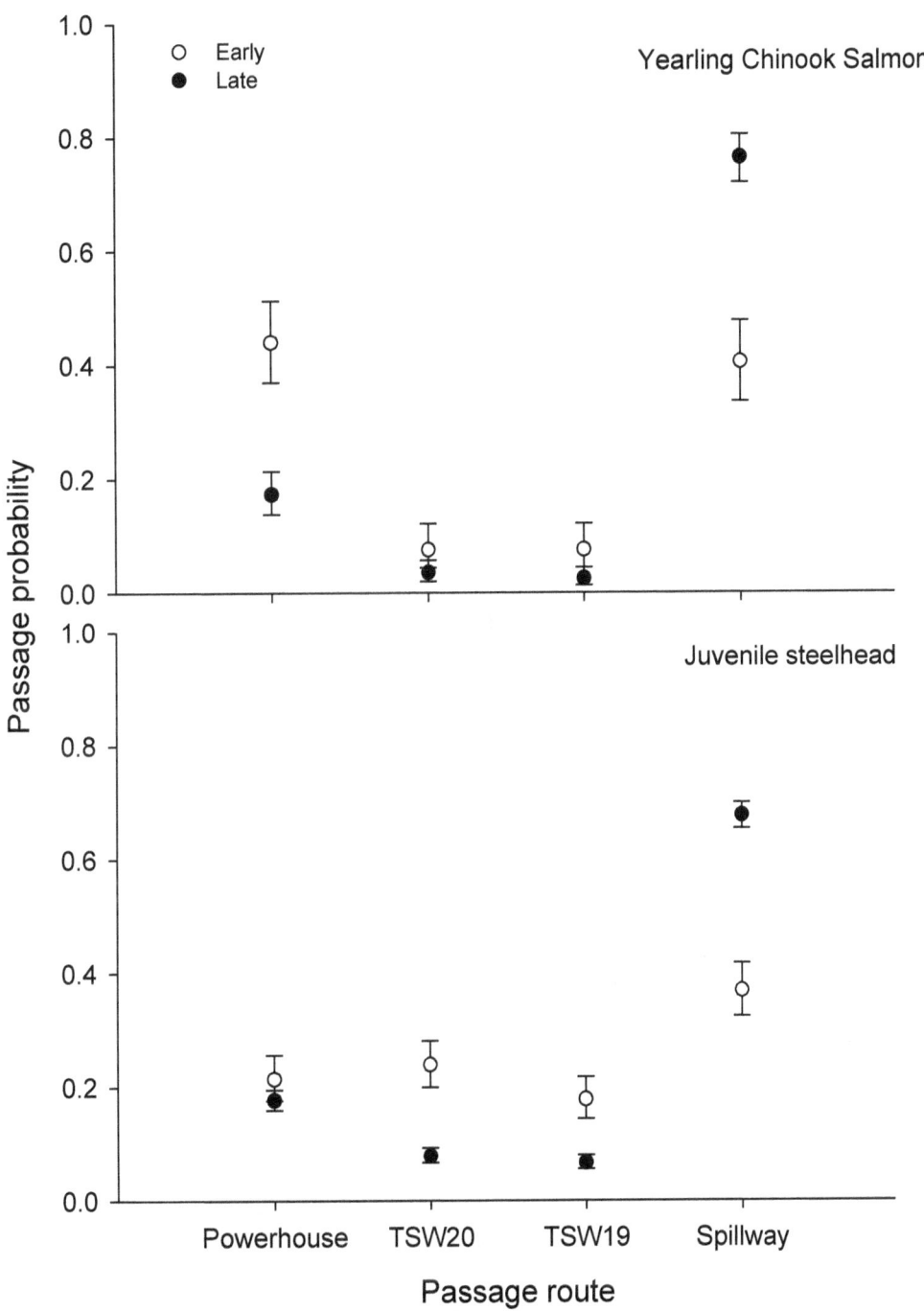

Figure 11. Graphs showing passage probabilities for acoustic-tagged yearling Chinook salmon and juvenile steelhead at McNary Dam presented by early (40 percent spill) and late (60 percent spill) periods during spring 2008. The early period was from April 30 to May 17, 2008, and the late period was from May 18 to June 12, 2008. Yearling Chinook salmon were released at Rocky Reach and Rock Island Dams and juvenile steelhead were released at Rocky Reach, Rock Island, Wanapum, and Priest Rapids Dams. Error bars represent the 95-percent profile likelihood confidence intervals.

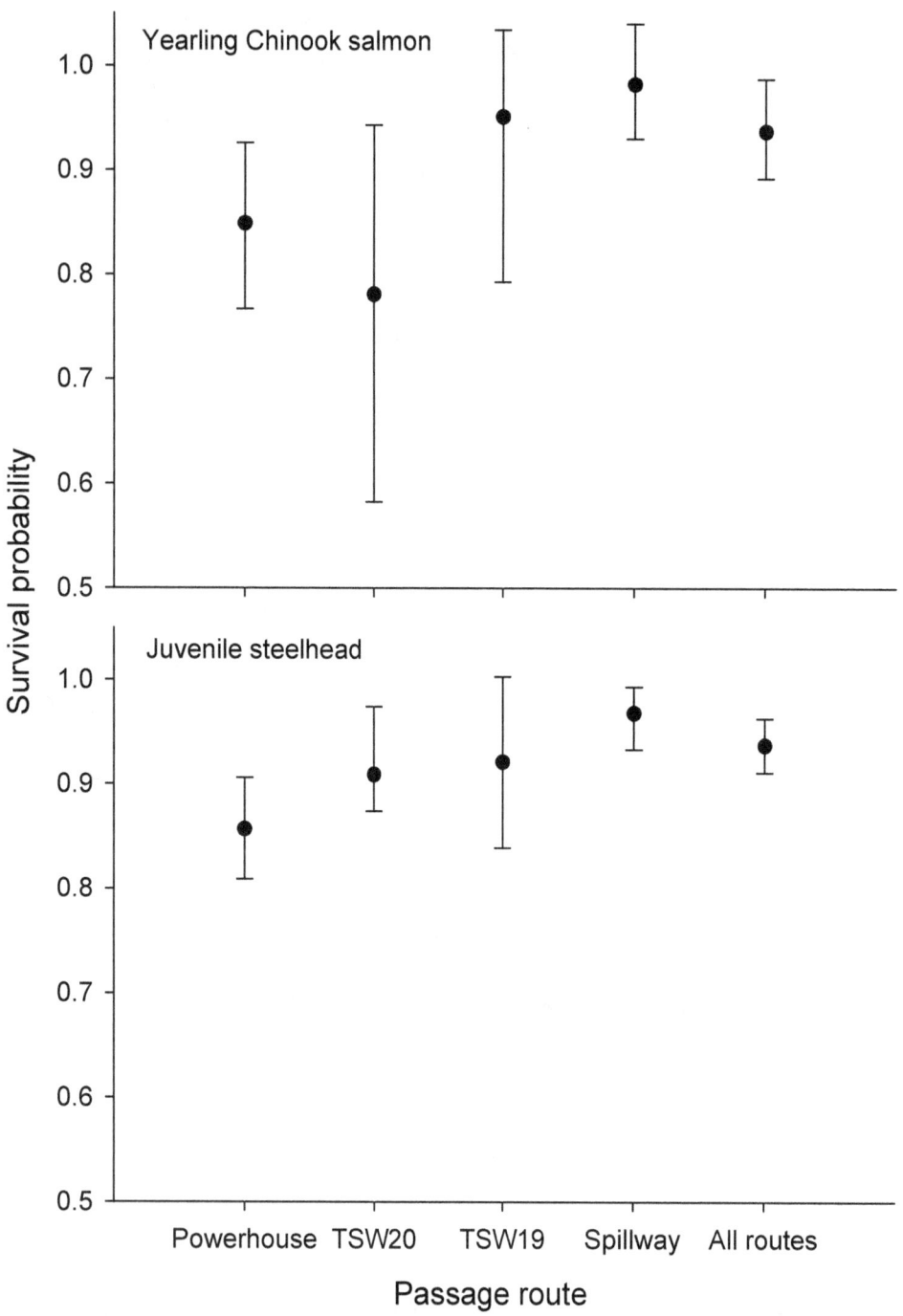

Figure 12. Graphs showing survival probabilities for acoustic-tagged yearling Chinook salmon and juvenile steelhead at McNary Dam during spring 2008. Yearling Chinook salmon were released at Rocky Reach and Rock Island Dams and juvenile steelhead were released at Rocky Reach, Rock Island, Wanapum, and Priest Rapids Dams. Error bars represent the 95-percent profile likelihood confidence intervals.

Table 9. Route-specific passage (*N*=1,891) and survival (single-release) probabilities for juvenile steelhead implanted with an acoustic tag, presented by early period (40 percent spill), late period (60 percent spill), and overall, spring 2008.

[The early period was from April 30 to May 17, 2008, and late period was from May 18 to June 17, 2008. Single-release estimates represent survival from passage at McNary Dam to Big Blalock Island located 24 kilometers downstream of McNary Dam. Fish were released at Priest Rapids, Rock Island, Rocky Reach, and Wanapum Dams. LCL, lower confidence limit; UCL, upper confidence limit; NA, not applicable]

Estimate (location)	Early Period (LCL,UCL)	Late Period (LCL,UCL)	Overall (LCL,UCL)
Passage probabilities			
Powerhouse	0.214 (0.176,0.256)	0.177 (0.159,0.195)	0.184 (0.168,0.201)
TSW 20	0.239 (0.199,0.281)	0.079 (0.067,0.093)	0.110 (0.097,0.124)
TSW 19	0.178 (0.144,0.217)	0.067 (0.056,0.080)	0.089 (0.077,0.101)
Spillway	0.369 (0.324,0.417)	0.677 (0.654,0.699)	0.617 (0.597,0.638)
Single-release survival probabilities			
Forebay	NA	NA	0.996 (0.987,1.004)
Powerhouse	0.892 (0.768,1.051)	0.847 (0.780,0.926)	0.857 (0.809,0.906)
TSW 20	0.907 (0.807,1.026)	0.909 (0.828,1.010)	0.909 (0.844, 0.971)
TSW 19	0.970 (0.849,1.125)	0.889 (0.790,1.019)	0.921 (0.839, 1.003)
Spillway	0.939 (0.863,1.026)	0.971 (0 0.935,1.011)	0.968 (0.933,0.993)
All routes	0.927 (0.877,0.983)	0.939 (0.909,0.970)	0.937 (0.911,0.963)

A subset of juvenile steelhead implanted with a PIT tag, in addition to an acoustic tag, enabled estimation of passage and survival probabilities for fish that passed through turbines, as well as for fish that passed through the juvenile bypass system. Passage probabilities for juvenile steelhead implanted with an acoustic and a PIT tag were similar to passage probabilities for juvenile steelhead implanted with only an acoustic tag (table 10). The passage route with the highest probability of passage was the spillway (0.699) followed by the juvenile bypass (0.122), the turbines (0.067), TSW 20 (0.064), and TSW 19 (0.048). Point estimates of survival were highest through TSW 20 (0.956), followed by the spillway (0.936), juvenile bypass (0.898), TSW 19 (0.822), and turbines (0.780), but all confidence intervals overlapped indicating there may have been little difference in the estimates. Forebay survival was high (1.007) and survival through all routes was 0.917. Fish guidance efficiency (FGE) for juvenile steelhead implanted with a PIT- and acoustic tag was 0.647 and fish passage efficiency (FPE) was 0.933.

Passage and survival probabilities for sockeye salmon were similar to the other species (table 11). The highest probability of passage (0.744) was at the spillway and also the highest survival (0.925). Probabilities of passage were relatively low for all other routes and survival ranged between 0.819 and 0.866 for the remaining routes. Forebay survival was 0.997 and survival through all routes was 0.907 for sockeye salmon.

Table 10. Route-specific passage (*N*=467) and survival (single-release) probabilities for the subset of juvenile steelhead implanted with an acoustic/PIT tag during spring 2008.

[Single-release estimates represent survival from passage at McNary Dam to Big Blalock Island located 24 kilometers downstream of McNary Dam. Fish were released at Priest Rapids, Rock Island, Rocky Reach, and Wanapum Dams. LCL, lower confidence limit; UCL, upper confidence limit; TSW, temporary spillway weir]

Estimate (location)	Juvenile Steelhead (LCL,UCL)
Passage probabilities	
Turbine	0.067 (0.048,0.090)
Bypass	0.122 (0.097,0.151)
TSW 20	0.064 (0.046,0.086)
TSW 19	0.048 (0.032,0.068)
Spillway	0.699 (0.660,0.736)
Fish guidance efficiency	0.647 (0.553,0.723)
Fish passage efficiency	0.933 (0.910,0.952)
Single-release survival probabilities	
Forebay	1.007 (0.985,1.025)
Turbine	0.780 (0.603,0.934)
Bypass	0.898 (0.777,1.005)
TSW 20	0.956 (0.801,1.073)
TSW 19	0.822 (0.618,0.987)
Spillway	0.936 (0.873,1.007)
All routes	0.917 (0.861,0.983)

Table 11. Route-specific passage (*N*=1,093) and survival (single-release) probabilities for sockeye salmon implanted with an acoustic tag, spring 2008.

[Sockeye salmon passed McNary Dam in 2008 only during the late period (May 18–June 21). Single-release estimates represent survival from passage at McNary Dam to Big Blalock Island located 24 kilometers downstream of McNary Dam. Sockeye salmon were released from May 13 to June 7, 2008, at Rock Island, Rocky Reach and Wells Dams. Additionally, sockeye salmon were released about halfway between Rock Island and Rocky Reach Dams. LCL, lower confidence limit; UCL, upper confidence limit; TSW, temporary spillway weir]

Estimate (location)	Sockeye Salmon (LCL,UCL)
Passage probabilities	
Powerhouse	0.189 (0.170,0.210)
TSW 20	0.021 (0.014,0.029)
TSW 19	0.045 (0.036,0.057)
Spillway	0.744 (0.721,0.765)
Single-release survival probabilities	
Forebay	0.997 (0.977,1.015)
Powerhouse	0.858 (0.795,0.922)
TSW 20	0.866 (0.680,1.009)
TSW 19	0.819 (0.689,0.932)
Spillway	0.925 (0.882,0.973)
All routes	0.907 (0.868,0.951)

Passage and Survival Probabilities in 2009

Route-specific passage and survival probabilities were estimated for the Mid-Columbia River released juvenile salmonids at McNary Dam during 2009 (tables 12, 13, and 14; figs. 13 and 14). A single release survival model was used to estimate survival from the specific routes and a weighted average of survival was used through all routes to a detection array 22 km downstream. The distance over which survival was estimated was slightly different than in our analyses of the 2008 data where estimates represent survival from passage to an array 24 km downstream (Big Blalock Island) of McNary Dam.

Passage probabilities for sockeye salmon were highest at the spillway (0.475), followed by the powerhouse (0.366), TSW 20 (0.123), and TSW 4 (0.036; table 12 and fig. 13). The same pattern existed for passage probabilities during day and night periods. Forebay survival was estimated at 1.00 and survival through all routes was 0.945. Over the entire season, the spillway provided the highest survival (0.959) of all available routes, followed by TSW 4 (0.945), TSW 20 (0.941), and the powerhouse (0.930; table 12 and fig. 14). During the day, survival was highest through TSW 4 (0.967), followed closely by the spillway (0.961), then TSW 20 (0.939) and the powerhouse (0.921; table 12). At night, the spillway had the highest survival (0.956), followed by the powerhouse (0.944), TSW 20 (0.943), and TSW 4 (0.930).

The highest probability of passage for steelhead released from the Mid-Columbia River at McNary Dam was through the powerhouse, both overall (0.367) and during the day (0.378; table 13 and fig. 13). However, TSW 20 was very efficient during the day (0.314) and overall (0.240) compared to TSW 4 (0.055). The highest probability of passage at night (0.402) and the second highest probability of passage overall (0.338) was through the spillway. Forebay survival of juvenile steelhead was estimated at 0.998 and survival through all routes was 0.954 which was very similar for sockeye salmon. Survival overall was highest at TSW 20 (0.981), followed by the spillway (0.968), the powerhouse (0.927) and TSW 4 (0.921; table 13 and fig.14). During the day, survival of juvenile steelhead was highest through TSW4 (1.000), followed by the spillway (0.990), TSW 20 (0.980), and the powerhouse (0.947). Survival at night followed the same pattern as the overall estimates. Survival at night was highest at TSW 20 (0.983), followed by the spillway (0.952), the powerhouse (0.905), and TSW 4 (0.889). Differences in survival between day and night generally were small (less than 0.040) with the exception of TSW 4 where survival during the day was 0.111 higher than during night.

A subset of juvenile steelhead implanted with a PIT tag, in addition to an acoustic tag, enabled estimation of passage and survival probabilities for fish that passed through turbines, as well as for fish that passed through the juvenile bypass system. Passage probabilities for juvenile steelhead implanted with an acoustic/PIT tag were nearly identical to passage probabilities for juvenile steelhead implanted with only an acoustic tag (table 14). The passage route with the highest probability of passage was the spillway (0.341) followed by the juvenile bypass (0.326), TSW 20 (0.238), TSW 4 (0.055), and the turbines (0.040). Survival was highest through TSW 20 (0.977) and the spillway (0.968), followed by the juvenile bypass (0.940), TSW 4 (0.917), and turbines (0.819). Forebay survival was 0.999 and survival through all routes was 0.952. FGE for juvenile steelhead implanted with a PIT/acoustic tag was 0.889 and FPE was 0.960.

Table 12. Route-specific passage (*N*=3,578) and survival (single-release) probabilities for sockeye salmon implanted with an acoustic tag, presented by day (0600–1759 hours), night (1800–0559 hours), and overall, spring 2009.

[Single-release estimates represent survival from passage at McNary Dam to Umatilla National Wildlife Refuge located 22 kilometers downstream of McNary Dam. Fish were released at Priest Rapids, Rock Island, Rocky Reach, Wanapum, and Wells Dams. LCL, lower confidence limit; UCL, upper confidence limit; TSW temporary spillway weir; NA, not applicable]

Estimate (location)	Day (LCL,UCL)	Night (LCL,UCL)	Overall (LCL,UCL)
Passage probabilities			
Powerhouse	0.387 (0.366,0.407)	0.338 (0.315,0.361)	0.366 (0.350,0.381)
TSW 20	0.122 (0.109,0.136)	0.124 (0.109,0.141)	0.123 (0.113,0.134)
TSW 4	0.026 (0.020,0.033)	0.051 (0.041,0.062)	0.036 (0.031,0.043)
Spillway	0.465 (0.444,0.486)	0.488 (0.464,0.512)	0.475 (0.459,0.491)
Single-release survival probabilities			
Forebay	NA	NA	1.000 (0.996,1.004)
Powerhouse	0.921 (0.896,0.942)	0.944 (0.923,0.961)	0.930 (0.913,0.944)
TSW 20	0.939 (0.906,0.964)	0.943 (0.906,0.970)	0.941 (0.917,0.957)
TSW 4	0.967 (0.897,0.996)	0.930 (0.862,0.972)	0.945 (0.898,0.971)
Spillway	0.961 (0.948,0.972)	0.956 (0.940,0.969)	0.959 (0.949,0.966)
All routes	0.943 (0.931,0.949)	0.949 (0.937,0.957)	0.945 (0.937,0.952)

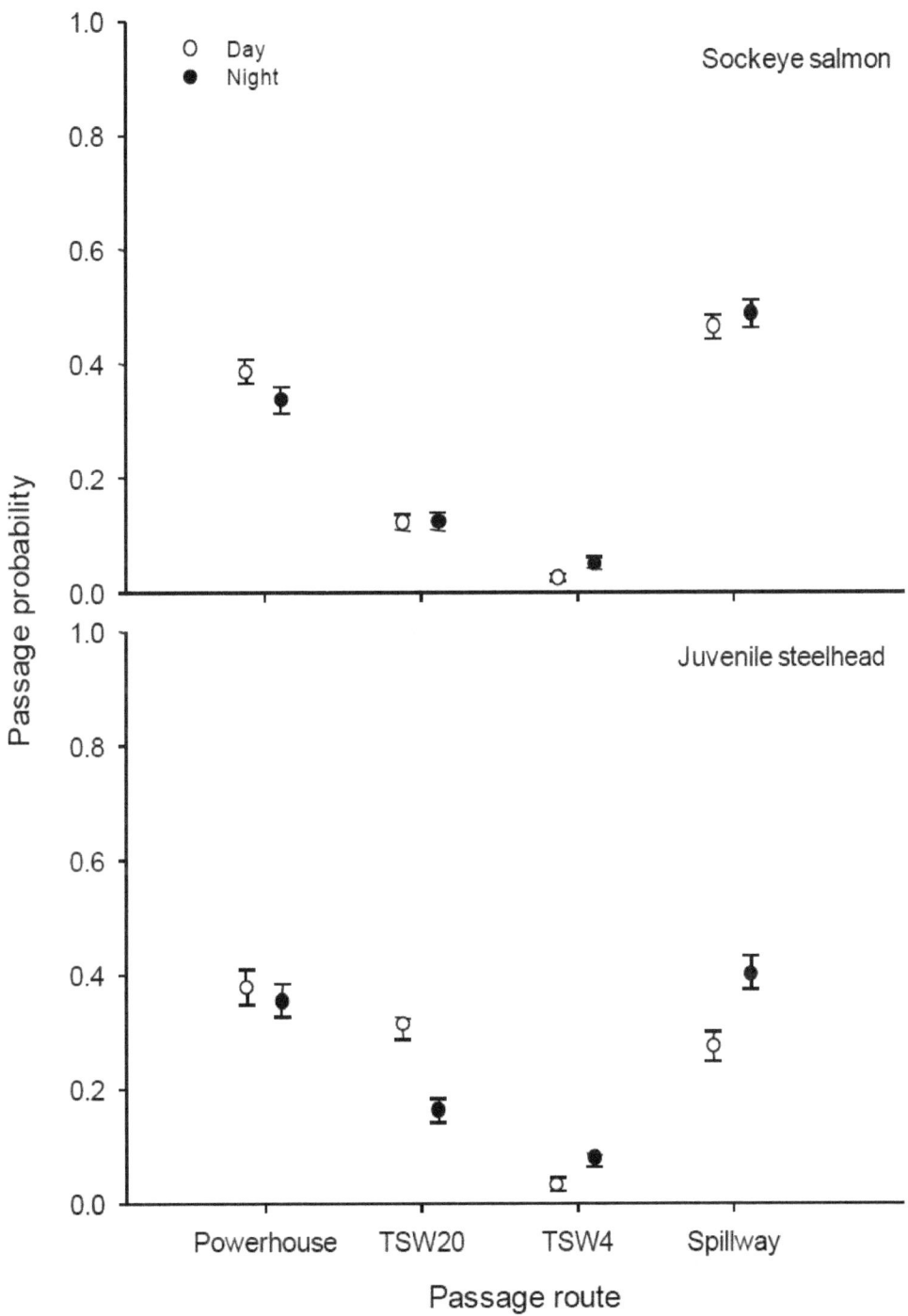

Figure 13. Graphs showing passage probabilities for acoustic-tagged sockeye salmon and juvenile steelhead at McNary Dam presented by day (0600–1759 hours) and night (1800–0559 hours) during spring 2009. Fish were released at Rocky Reach, Rock Island, Wanapum, and Priest Rapids Dams. Additionally, sockeye salmon were released at Wells Dam. Error bars represent the 95-percent profile likelihood confidence intervals.

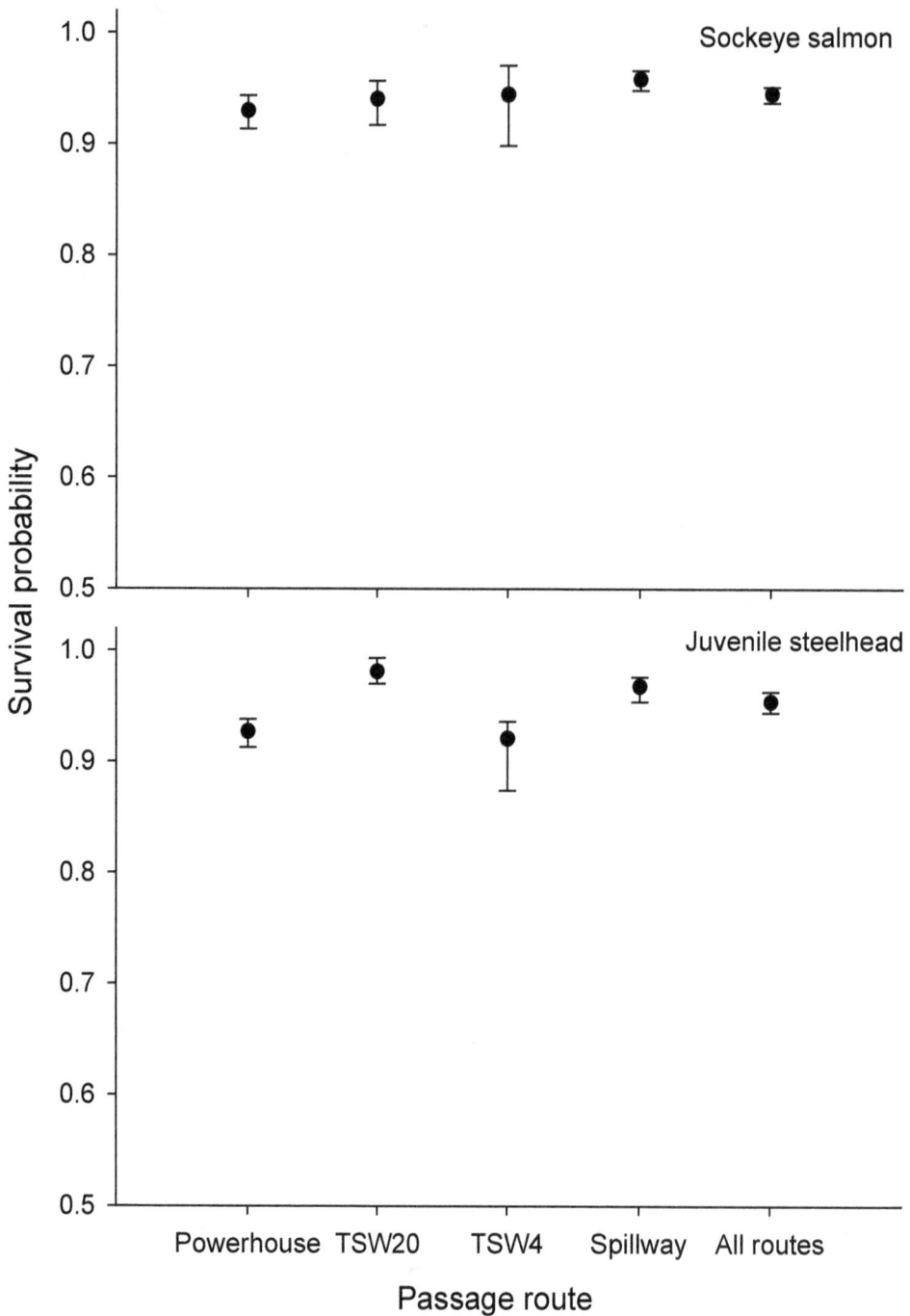

Figure 14. Graphs showing survival probabilities for acoustic-tagged sockeye salmon and juvenile steelhead at McNary Dam during spring 2009. Fish were released at Priest Rapids, Rock Island, Rocky Reach, and Wanapum Dams. Additionally, sockeye salmon were released at Wells Dam. Error bars represent the 95-percent profile likelihood confidence intervals.

Table 13. Route-specific passage (*N*=1,860) and survival (single-release) probabilities for juvenile steelhead implanted with an acoustic tag, presented by day (0600–1759 hours), night (1800–0559 hours), and overall, spring 2009.

[Single-release estimates represent survival from passage at McNary Dam to Umatilla National Wildlife Refuge located 22 kilometers downstream of McNary Dam. Fish were released at Priest Rapids, Rock Island, Rocky Reach, and Wanapum Dams. LCL, lower confidence limit; UCL, upper confidence limit; TSW, temporary spillway weir; NA, not applicable]

Estimate (location)	Day (LCL,UCL)	Night (LCL,UCL)	Overall (LCL,UCL)
Passage probabilities			
Powerhouse	0.378 (0.349,0.409)	0.354 (0.325,0.384)	0.367 (0.353,0.385)
TSW 20	0.314 (0.286,0.324)	0.164 (0.142,0.184)	0.240 (0.229,0.259)
TSW 4	0.032 (0.022,0.044)	0.080 (0.065,0.085)	0.055 (0.046,0.065)
Spillway	0.276 (0.249,0.299)	0.402 (0.373,0.432)	0.338 (0.318,0.358)
Single-release survival probabilities			
Forebay	NA	NA	0.998 (0.992,1.003)
Powerhouse	0.947 (0.910,0.974)	0.905 (0.873,0.933)	0.927 (0.913,0.938)
TSW 20	0.980 (0.958,0.995)	0.983 (0.955,0.997)	0.981 (0.970,0.993)
TSW 4	[1]1.000	0.889 (0.808,0.946)	[2]0.921 (0.874,0.936)
Spillway	0.990 (0.970,1.002)	0.952 (0.928,0.970)	0.968 (0.954,0.976)
All routes	[2]0.971 (0.959,0.984)	0.936 (0.920,0.947)	[2]0.954 (0.944,0.963)

[1] Survival probability and confidence limits could not be estimated using maximum likelihood methods because 100 percent (33/33) of the fish were detected passing this route at downstream detection arrays. Although the modeling software could not produce an estimate, the best estimate of survival is 100 percent.

[2]Variance from parameter in footnote 1 not accounted for in other estimates derived from this parameter.

Table 14. Route-specific passage (*N*=1,702) and survival (single-release) probabilities for juvenile steelhead implanted with an acoustic/PIT tag during spring 2009.

[Single-release estimates represent survival from passage at McNary Dam to Umatilla National Wildlife Refuge located 22 kilometers downstream of McNary Dam. Juvenile steelhead were released from May 2 to 25, 2009, at Priest Rapids, Rock Island, and Wanapum Dams. LCL, lower confidence limit; UCL, upper confidence limit; TSW, temporary spillway weir]

Estimate (location)	Juvenile Steelhead (LCL,UCL)
Passage probabilities	
Turbine	0.040 (0.032,0.050)
Bypass	0.326 (0.305,0.347)
TSW 20	0.238 (0.219,0.258)
TSW 4	0.055 (0.045,0.066)
Spillway	0.341 (0.319,0.362)
Fish guidance efficiency	0.889 (0.865,0.911)
Fish passage efficiency	0.960 (0.950,0.968)
Single-release survival probabilities	
Forebay	0.999 (0.992,1.003)
Turbine	0.819 (0.722,0.896)
Bypass	0.940 (0.914,0.961)
TSW 20	0.977 (0.960,0.990)
TSW 4	0.917 (0.852,0.961)
Spillway	0.968 (0.952,0.981)
All routes	0.952 (0.947,0.956)

Discussion

We successfully were able to assess survival of acoustic-tagged juvenile salmonids passing McNary Dam that were released by Grant and Chelan County PUDs in the Mid-Columbia River. These post-hoc analyses were possible because the USGS was contracted by the Walla Walla District Army Corps of Engineers to install equipment to detect acoustic-tagged fish released by the USGS from Hat Rock State Park (8 km upstream) for survival studies at McNary Dam in 2008 and 2009. The presence of the detection systems at McNary Dam and the ability of these systems to detect the tags used in the Mid-Columbia River studies allowed the USGS to estimate survival and passage probabilities for Mid-Columbia River released acoustic-tagged juvenile salmonids at McNary Dam.

Although we discuss differences and similarities between the results from Mid-Columbia River released fish and fish released near Hat Rock State Park, located upstream of McNary Dam (Adams and Liedtke 2009, 2010), these comparisons were not part of either study plan and differences between the studies may confound direct comparisons made between the Mid-Columbia and McNary release groups. Potential confounding factors include differences in (1) the source of the test fish, (2) tagging and release protocols, (3) annual dam operations and configurations, (4) how the survival models were constructed (that is, number of routes estimable given the number of fish detected), and (5) the number and length of reaches included in the analysis (downstream reach length and arrays). These caveats aside, we believe it is still worthwhile to examine and discuss general trends among the various release groups to provide insight into the passage and survival of a group of fish that would otherwise be unattainable.

During 2008, the passage probability of fish passing through the spillway was higher for all species released from the Mid-Columbia River than for fish released near Hat Rock State Park (figs. 15, 16, and 17). For all other routes, probabilities of passage were higher for fish released at Hat Rock State Park than for fish released at the Mid-Columbia River. These differences could be explained by the timing of passage of each group. Most mid-Columbia fish (81–100 percent) passed McNary Dam during the 60 percent spill and most Hat Rock-released fish passed during the 40 percent spill. Because a high proportion of the Mid-Columbia fish passed during high spillway discharge, fish were more likely to pass through spill. Conversely, because a high proportion of Hat Rock fish passed during low spillway discharge, the probability of passing through non-spill routes was high for these fish. Point estimates of survival probabilities were lower for Mid-Columbia released fish than for Hat Rock released fish and were highly variable for all species and for all routes with two exceptions: Yearling Chinook salmon passing through the spillway and TSW 19 (figs. 16 and 18). However, low detection probabilities (30–50 percent) and small sample size of Mid-Columbia released fish resulted in relatively high variance about the point estimates. The high variance resulted in overlap of the confidence intervals for all survival estimates, indicating there may have been little difference in survival between release groups. In addition to the relatively small number of sockeye salmon detected, the tag failure rate was high for the transmitter for these fish (about 8 percent, appendix C), which could potentially bias the results. Nonetheless, the high variance observed likely would mask any tag bias effects. We also cannot discern whether any differences in survival estimates are a result of direct mortality at the dam or of potential indirect effects such as a prolonged period since being tagged, prolonged travel time, varying tag life, or other potential handling and source differences between release groups. Despite this, we note that the similarity of estimates between release groups provides valuable information and indicates that increased migration time or migration distance likely are not causing any differences in survival.

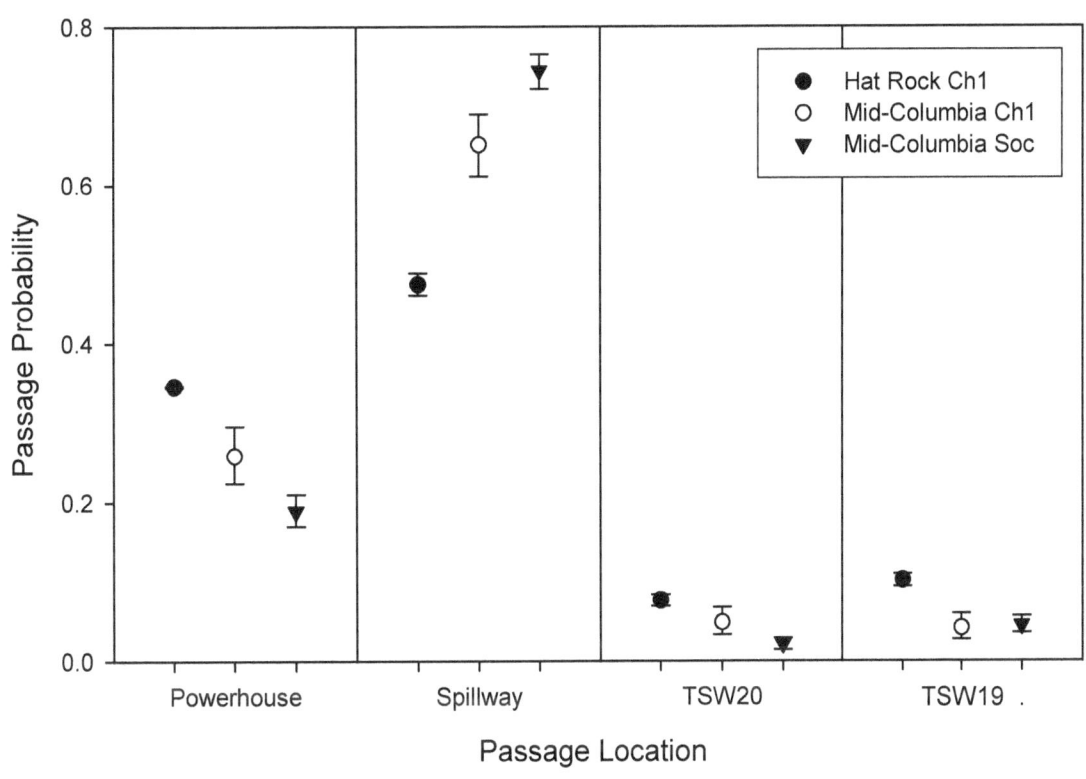

Figure 15. Graph showing passage probabilities for Mid-Columbia River released yearling Chinook salmon (Ch1, open circles), sockeye salmon (Soc, black triangles), and Hat Rock released yearling Chinook salmon (Ch1, black circles) through individual passage locations at McNary Dam, 2008. The powerhouse encompasses both the turbine and bypass routes combined. Error bars represent the 95-percent profile likelihood confidence intervals.

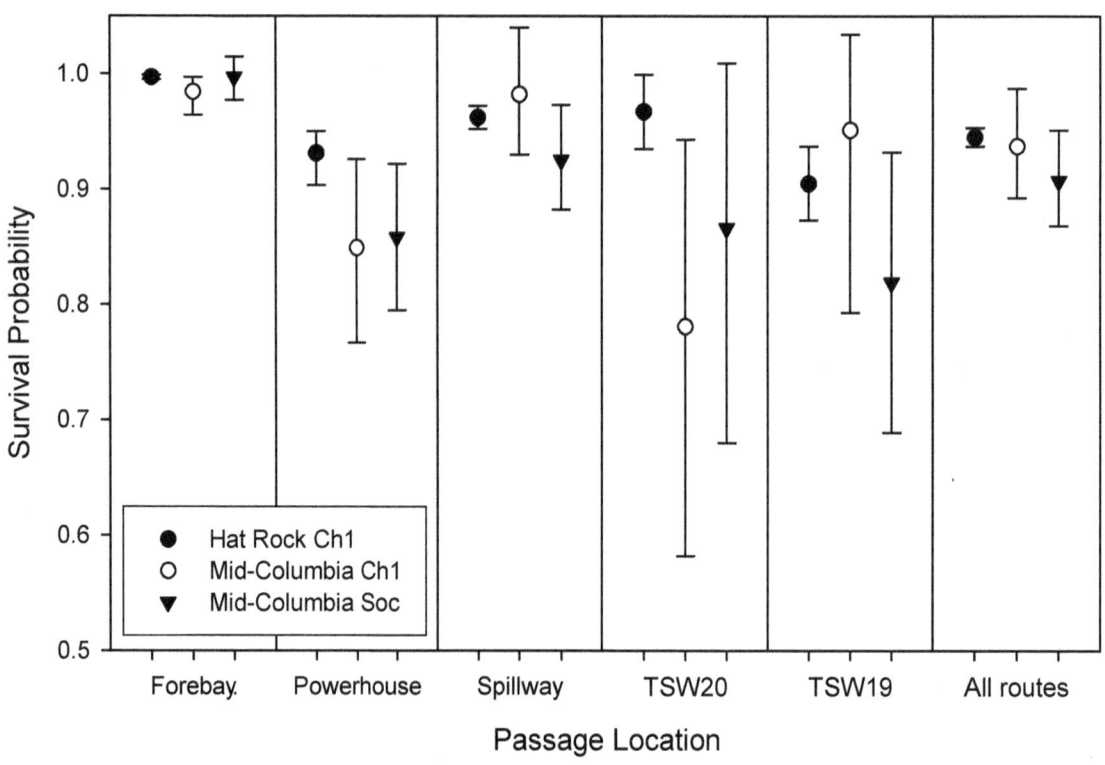

Figure 16. Graph showing survival probabilities for Mid-Columbia River released yearling Chinook salmon (Ch1, open circles), sockeye salmon (Soc, black triangles), and Hat Rock released yearling Chinook salmon (Ch1, black circles) through individual passage locations at McNary Dam, 2008 using a single release model from McNary Dam to 24 kilometers downstream. The powerhouse encompasses both the turbine and bypass routes combined. Error bars represent the 95-percent profile likelihood confidence intervals.

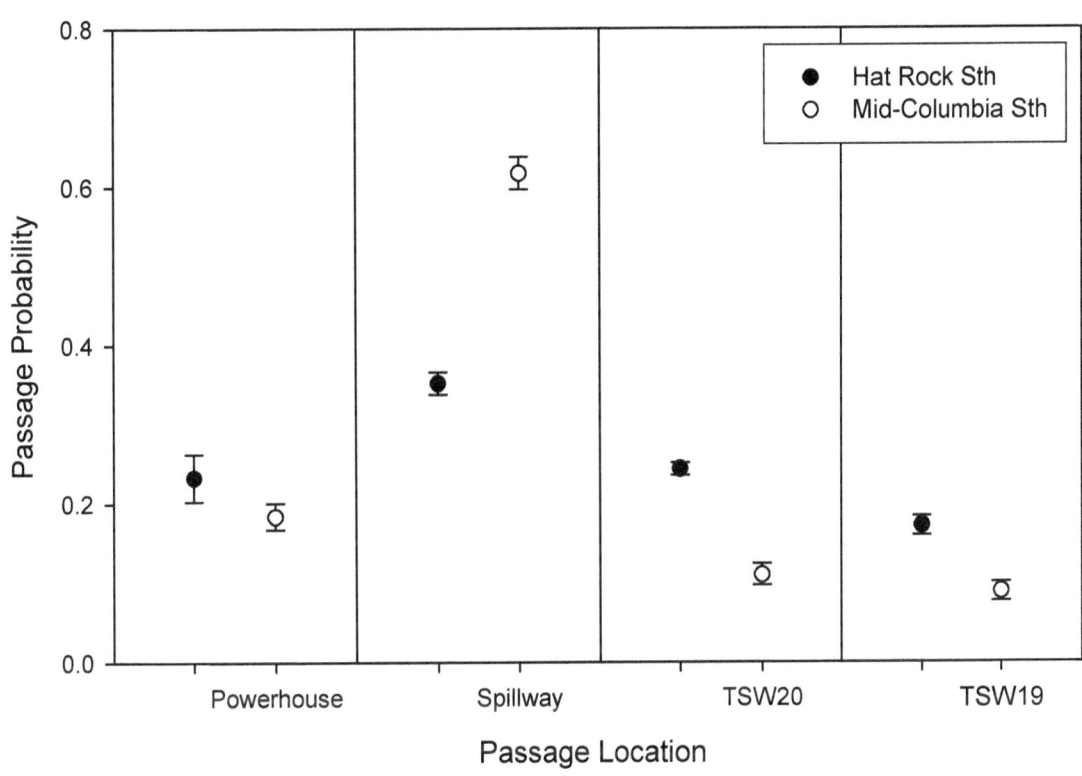

Figure 17. Graph showing passage probabilities for juvenile steelhead (Sth) released from the Mid-Columbia River (open circles) and Hat Rock State Park (black circles) through individual passage locations at McNary Dam, 2008. The powerhouse encompasses both the turbine and bypass routes combined. Error bars represent the 95-percent profile likelihood confidence intervals.

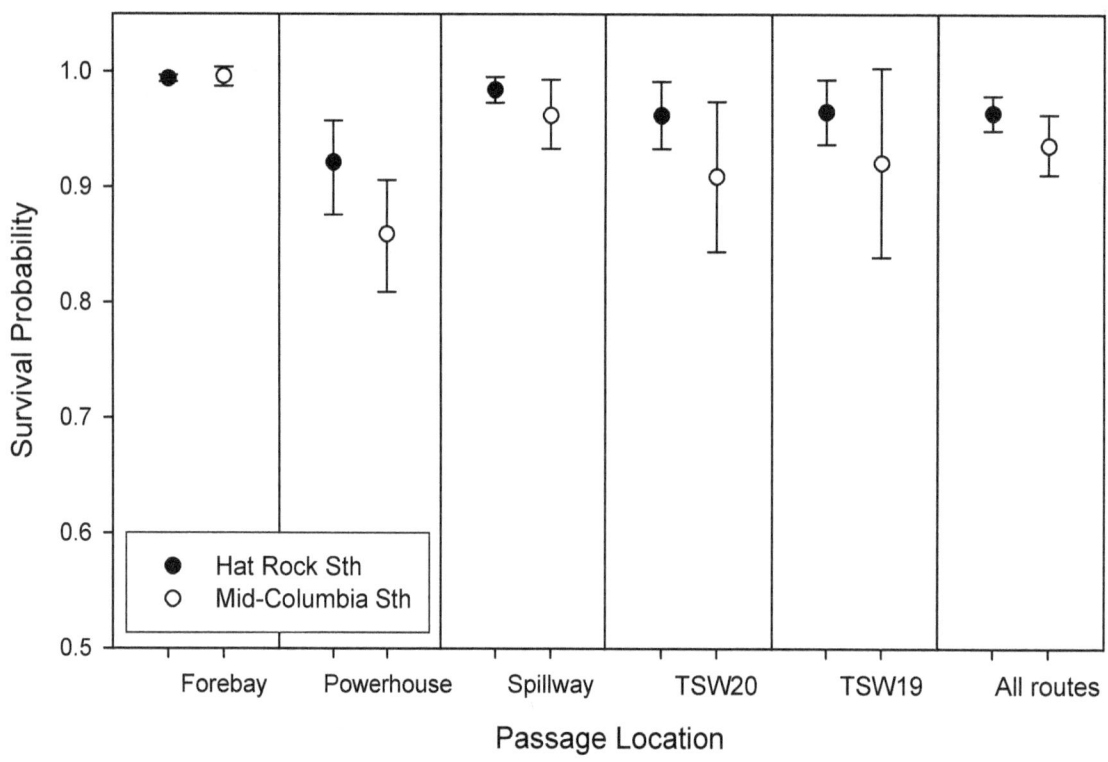

Figure 18. Graph showing survival probabilities for juvenile steelhead (Sth) released from the Mid-Columbia River (open circles) and Hat Rock State Park (black circles) through individual passage locations at McNary Dam, 2008 using a single release model from McNary Dam to 24 kilometers downstream. The powerhouse encompasses both the turbine and bypass routes combined. Error bars represent the 95-percent profile likelihood confidence intervals.

During 2009, passage probabilities within routes generally were very similar for the Mid-Columbia River released fish and the Hat Rock released fish. Between routes, for both salmon and juvenile steelhead release groups, most fish passed through the powerhouse and spillway (probabilities were similar between powerhouse and spillway) followed by TSW 20 and TSW 4 (figs. 19, 20, and 21). Although the probabilities of passage were lower for individual TSWs (3–23 percent) than for the powerhouse (37–39 percent) or spillway (33–48 percent), when combined the two TSWs accounted for 16–35 percent of fish passage. Survival estimates by route and all routes combined were nearly identical among release groups and species (figs. 20 and 22). Although differences were slight in point estimates for some routes, confidence intervals overlapped, likely indicating no difference in the estimates of survival.

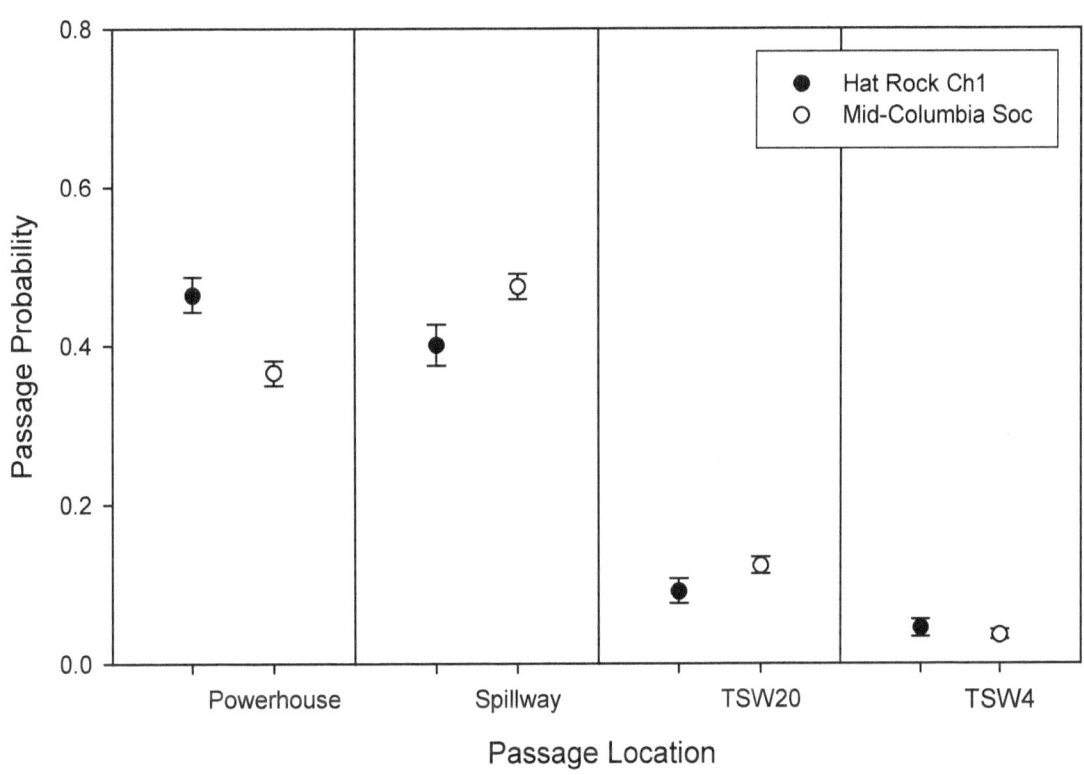

Figure 19. Graph showing passage probabilities for Mid-Columbia River released sockeye salmon (Soc, open circles) and Hat Rock released yearling Chinook salmon (Ch1, black circles) through individual passage locations at McNary Dam, 2009. The powerhouse encompasses both the turbine and bypass routes combined. Error bars represent the 95-percent profile likelihood confidence intervals.

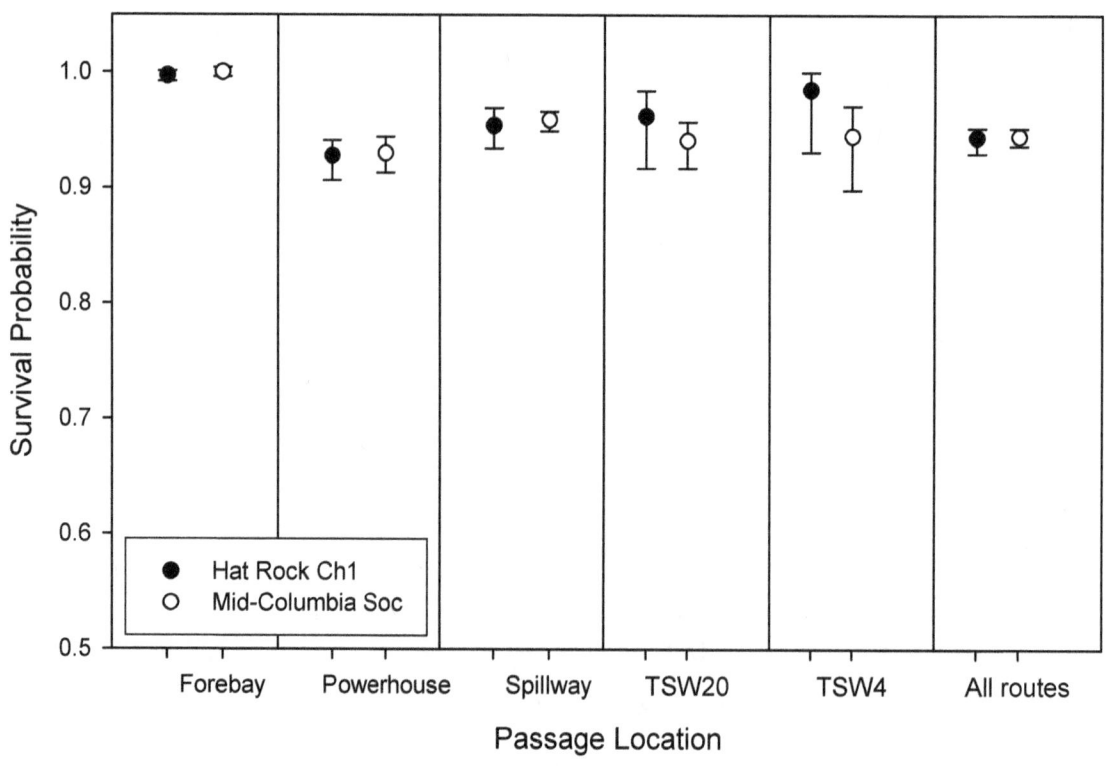

Figure 20. Graph showing survival probabilities for Mid-Columbia River released sockeye salmon (Soc, open circles) and Hat Rock released yearling Chinook salmon (Ch1, black circles) through individual passage locations at McNary Dam, 2009, using a single release model from McNary Dam to 22 kilometers downstream. The powerhouse encompasses both the turbine and bypass routes combined. Error bars represent the 95-percent profile likelihood confidence intervals.

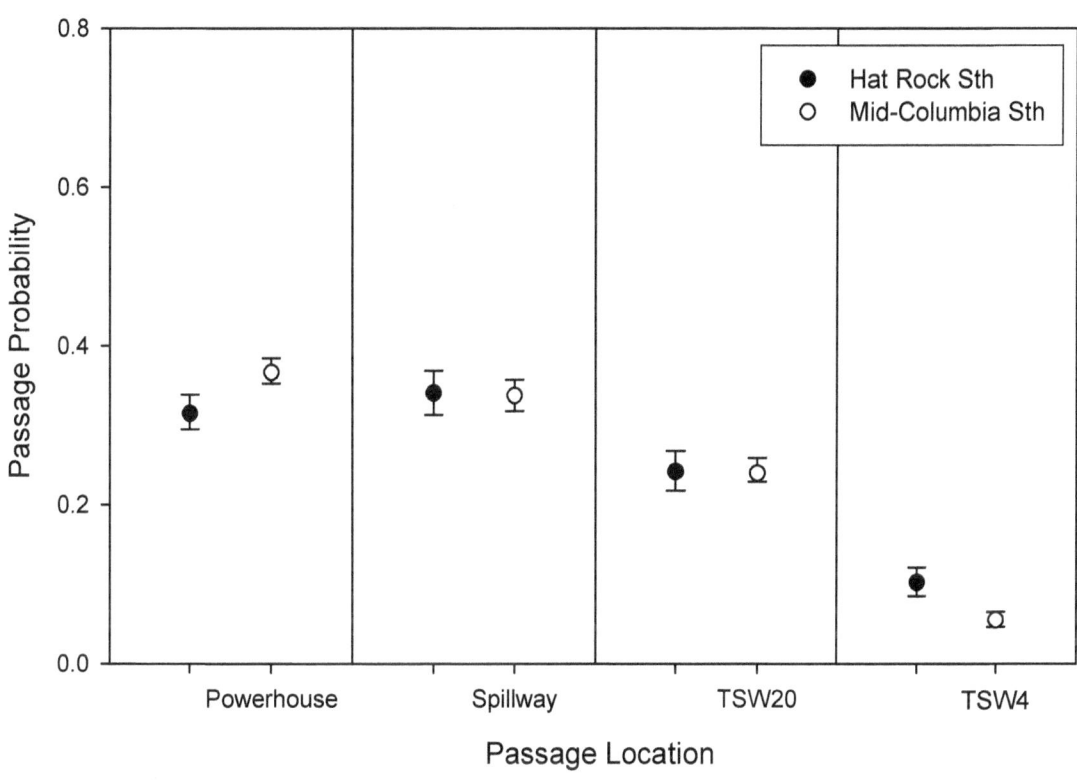

Figure 21. Graph showing passage probabilities for juvenile steelhead (Sth) released from the Mid-Columbia River (open circles) and Hat Rock State Park (black circles) through individual passage locations at McNary Dam, 2009. The powerhouse encompasses both the turbine and bypass routes combined. Error bars represent the 95-percent profile likelihood confidence intervals.

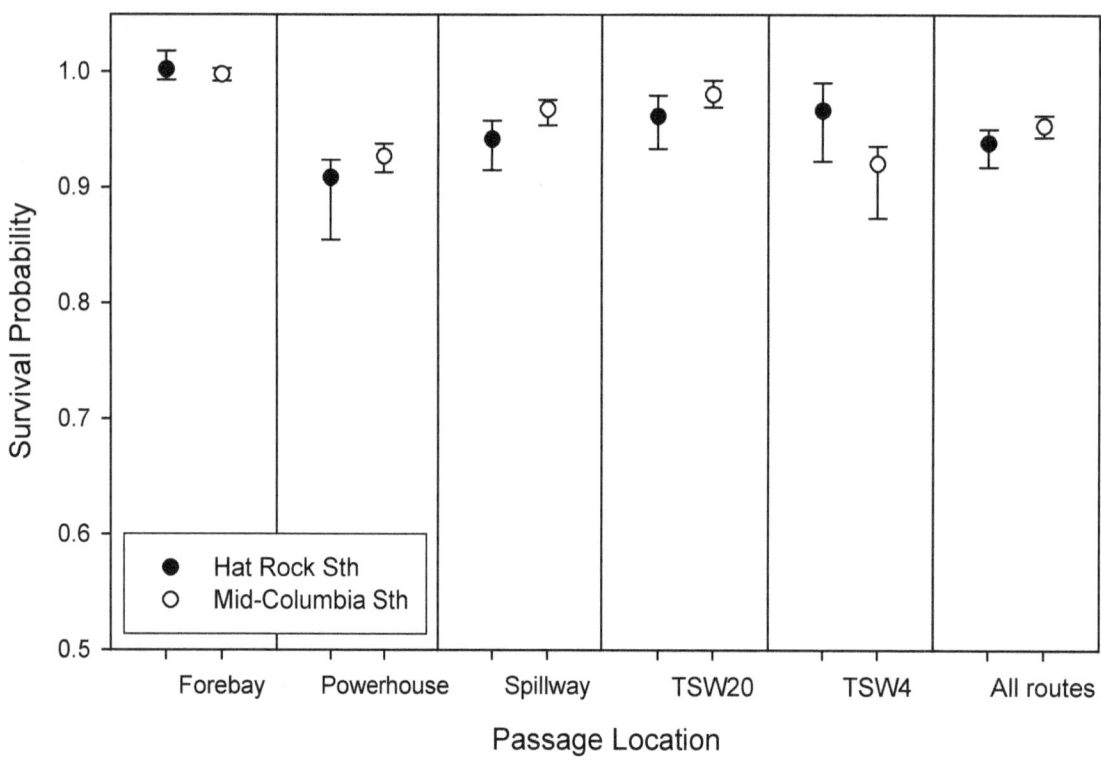

Figure 22. Graph showing survival probabilities for juvenile steelhead (Sth) released from the Mid-Columbia River (open circles) and Hat Rock State Park (black circles) through individual passage locations at McNary Dam, 2009 using a single release model from McNary Dam to 22 kilometers downstream. The powerhouse encompasses both the turbine and bypass routes combined. Error bars represent the 95-percent profile likelihood confidence intervals.

The configuration and operation of McNary Dam changed between 2008 and 2009. A change in configuration included the location of TSW design 1 being in spill bay 19 during 2008 and in spill bay 4 during spring 2009. We observed increased passage probabilities of 10–13 percent in 2009 compared to 2008 for all species passing through TSW design 2. However, passage probabilities declined 1–3 percent for fish passing through TSW design 1 in 2009, compared to 2008. Point estimates of survival were 5 and 7 percent higher in 2009 than in 2008 for juvenile steelhead and sockeye salmon, respectively, passing through TSW design 2. For fish passing through TSW design 1, survival was 12 percent higher in 2009 than in 2008 for sockeye salmon, but similar for steelhead. However, confidence intervals were very large for TSW survival estimates in 2008. Unlike Mid-Columbia released steelhead, the passage probabilities and survival through the TSWs were very similar for Hat Rock released steelhead in 2008 and 2009, regardless of TSW design. Operationally, mean total discharge was greater in 2008 (320.5 thousand ft³/s) than in 2009 (277.3 thousand ft³/s), and a greater proportion of water was discharged through the spillway and TSWs in 2008 (mean = 51 percent) than in 2009 (mean = 45 percent). The difference in either the proportion of project discharge spilled or simply the total volume spilled in 2008 compared to 2009 likely explains the higher passage probability for all species and release groups for the spillway in 2008, as well as the higher probability of passage through the powerhouse for both juvenile steelhead and sockeye salmon in 2009. Although most juvenile steelhead in 2009 passed through the powerhouse, based on the subset of PIT-tagged juvenile steelhead, most (89 percent) of those fish were guided away from the turbines and into the juvenile fish facility. Because no sockeye salmon received PIT tags, we could not separate guided from unguided fish, and therefore could not estimate FGE for sockeye salmon. Given the scope of this study, it was very difficult to account for all of the differences that potentially existed between years and release groups. Consequently, our ability to make comparisons across years and among study groups is confounded because of differences in fish source, acoustic tags, tagging and release protocols, dam operations and configurations, the nature of the branching models used (number of routes estimable given the number of fish detected), and the number and length of reaches evaluated (downstream reach length and arrays). Despite this, we conclude that the information we provide in this report can help to develop testable hypotheses and insight into strategies for processing and analyzing data using fish released from disparate locations and studies. Our results also suggest that survival results for fish that have been tagged for long periods and traveled great distances was similar to survival results for fish that had been tagged for short time periods and traveled relatively short distances. Our results also indicate that sockeye salmon follow similar passage and survival trends as yearling Chinook salmon.

Acknowledgments

We thank Ann Setter, Brad Eby, Bill Prewitt, and individuals in the U.S. Army Corps of Engineers for their cooperation and assistance on the project. We also thank Grant and Chelan County PUDs, Hydroacoustic Technology Inc., and Blueleaf Environmental for sharing their data. Without their cooperation and hard work, this analysis could not be performed. Further, we thank Leah Sullivan and Tracey Steig for being so helpful with the data and information sharing process. We also greatly appreciate the U.S. Coast Guard, the U.S. Fish and Wildlife Service, the Portland District of the U.S. Army Corps of Engineers, and the Washington Department of Transportation for permission to install acoustic telemetry equipment on their property. We thank all of our colleagues at the Columbia River Research Laboratory for their assistance and dedication. Funding for this project was provided by the U.S. Army Corps of Engineers, Walla Walla District, Washington, Contract W68SBV90070150.

References Cited

Adams, N.S., and Liedtke, T.L., eds., 2009, Juvenile salmonid survival, passage, and egress at McNary Dam during tests of temporary spillway weirs, 2008: Anadromous Fish Evaluation Program, U.S. Army Corps of Engineers Report 2008-W68SBV80448890.

Adams, N.S., and Liedtke, T.L., eds., 2010, Juvenile salmonid survival, passage, and egress at McNary Dam during tests of temporary spillway weirs, 2009: Anadromous Fish Evaluation Program, U.S. Army Corps of Engineers Report 2009-W68SBV90070150.

Adams, N.S., Plumb, J.M., Hatton, T.W., Jones, E.C., Swyers, N.M., Sholtis, M.D., Reagan, R.E., and Cash, K.M., 2008, Survival and migration behavior of juvenile salmonids at McNary Dam, 2006: Anadromous Fish Evaluation Program, U.S. Army Corps of Engineers Report 2006-W68SBV60478899.

Burnham, K.P., Anderson, D.R., White, G.C., Brownie, C., and Pollock, K.H., 1987, Design and Analysis Methods for Fish Survival Experiments Based on Release-Recapture: American Fisheries Society Monograph 5.

Cormack, R.M., 1964, Estimates of survival from the sighting of marked animals: Biometrika, v. 51, p. 429–438.

Cowen, L., and Schwarz, C.J., 2005, Capture-recapture studies using radio telemetry with premature radio-tag failure: Biometrics, v. 61, p. 657–664.

Fish Passage Center, 2010, Fish Passage Center website, accessed April 8, 2010, at http://www.fpc.org/smolt/historicsmpsubmitdata.html.

Giorgi, A.E., Hillman, T.W., and Stevenson, J.R., 1997, Factors that influence that downstream migration rates of juvenile salmon and juvenile steelhead through the hydroelectric system in the mid-Columbia River Basin: North American Journal of Fisheries Management, v. 17, p. 268–282.

Hardiman, J.M., Walker, C.E., Jones, E.C., Counihan, T.D., and Adams, N.S., 2009, Assessing survival for Mid-Columbia River released juvenile salmonids at McNary Dam in 2006 and 2007: Anadromous Fish Evaluation Program, U.S. Army Corps of Engineers Report 2008-W68SBV80448890.

Jolly, G.M., 1965, Explicit estimates from capture-recapture data with both death and immigration-stochastic model: Biometrika, v. 52, p. 225–247.

Lady, J.M., and Skalski. J.R., 2009, USER 4—User specified estimation routine: Seattle, Wash., School of Aquatic and Fishery Sciences (also available at http://www.cbr.washington.edu/paramest/user/.)

Lebreton, J.D., Burnham, K.P., Clobert, J., and Anderson, D.R., 1992, Modeling survival and testing biological hypotheses using marked animals—A unified approach with case studies: Ecological Monographs 62, p. 67–118.

Mesa, M.G., 1994, Effects of multiple acute stressors on the predator avoidance ability and physiology of juvenile Chinook salmon: Transactions of the American Fisheries Society 123, p. 786–793.

Plumb, J.M., Perry, R.W., Adams, N.S., and Rondorf, D.W., 2006, The effects of river impoundment and hatchery rearing on the migration behavior of juvenile steelhead in the Lower Snake River, Washington: North American Journal of Fisheries Management, v. 26, p. 438–452.

Raymond, H.L., 1968, Migration rates of hatchery Chinook salmon in relation to flows and impoundments in the Columbia and Snake Rivers: Transactions of the American Fisheries Society, v. 97, 356–359.

Raymond, H.L., 1979, Effects of dams and impounds on migrations of juvenile Chinook salmon and juvenile steelhead from the Snake River, 1966 to 1975: Transactions of the American Fisheries Society, v. 108, p. 505–529.

Seber, G.A.F., 1965, A note on the multiple recapture census: Biometrika, v. 52, p. 249–259.

Skalski, J.R., Stevenson, J.R., Lady, J., Townsend, R., Giorgi, A.E., Miller, M., and English, K.E., 2001, An assessment of project, pool, and dam survival for Chinook and juvenile steelhead smolts at Rocky Reach and Rock Island dams using radio telemetry and PIT-tag techniques, 2000: Columbia Basin Research to Chelan County Public Utility District Report.

Skalski, J.R., Townsend, R., Lady, J., Giorgi, A.E., Stevenson, J.R., and McDonald, R.S., 2002, Estimating route-specific passage and survival probabilities at a hydroelectric project from smolt radio telemetry studies: Canadian Journal of Fisheries and Aquatic Sciences, v. 59, p. 1385–1393.

Steig, T.W., Nealson, P.A., Kumagai, K.K., Rowdon, B.J., Selleck J.R., and McFadden, B.D., 2009, Route specific passage of juvenile Chinook, sockeye and juvenile steelhead salmon using acoustic tag methodologies at Rocky Reach and Rock Island Dams in 2008: Final report for Chelan County Public Utility District No. 1 by Hydroacoustic Technology.

Steig, T.W., Nealson, P.A., Kumagai, K.K., Rowdon, B.J., Selleck, J.R., and Tunnicliffe, C., 2010, Route specific passage of juvenile Chinook, sockeye and juvenile steelhead salmon using acoustic tag methodologies at Rocky Reach and Rock Island Dams in 2009: Final report for Chelan County Public Utility District No. 1 by Hydroacoustic Technology.

Stevenson, J.R., Skalski, J.R., Lady, J., Townsend, R., Giorgi, A.E., and McDonald, R., 2000, A pilot study assessing the feasibility of using radio telemetry and PIT-tag techniques to estimate project, pool, and dam survival of juvenile steelhead smolts at Rocky Reach and Rock Island dams, 1999: Report to Chelan County Public Utility District No. 1 by BioAnalysts.

Sullivan, L.S., Wright, C.D., Rizor, S.E., Timko, M.A., Fitzgerald, C.A., Meagher, M.L., Skalski, J.R., and Townsend, R.L., 2008, Analysis of juvenile Chinook, juvenile steelhead and sockeye salmon behavior using acoustic tags at Wanapum and Priest Rapids dams, 2008: Draft report for Grant County Public Utility District No. 2 by Hydroacoustic Technology.

Timko, M.A., Sullivan, L.S., Wright, C.D., Rizor, S.E., O'Connor, R.R., Skalski, J.R., Townsend, R.L., Fitzgerald, C.A., Meagher, M.M., Kukes, T.J., and Stephenson, J.D., 2010, Behavior and survival analysis of juvenile steelhead and sockeye through the Priest Rapids Hydroelectric Project in 2009: Final report for Grant County Public Utility District No. 2 by Blue Leaf Environmental.

Townsend, R.L., Skalski, J.R., Dillingham, P., and Steig, T.W., 2006, Correcting bias in survival estimation resulting from tag failure in acoustic and radio telemetry studies: Journal of Agricultural, Biological, and Environmental Statistics, v. 11, p. 183–196.

Whitney, R.R., Calvin, L.D., Erho, M.W., Jr., and Coutant, C.C., 1997, Downstream passage for salmon at hydroelectric projects in the Columbia River Basin—Development, installation, and evaluation: Northwest Power Planning Council Report No. 97–15.

Zabel, R.W., 1994, Spatial and temporal models of migrating juvenile salmon with applications: Seattle, Wash., University of Washington, Ph.D. dissertation.

Zabel, R.W., 2002, Using "travel time" data to characterize the behavior of migrating animals: The American Naturalist, v. 159, p. 372–387.

Zabel, R.W., and Anderson, J.J.,1997, A model of the travel time of migrating juvenile salmon, with an application to Snake River spring Chinook salmon: North American Journal of Fisheries Management, v. 17, p. 93–100.

Glossary

CH1	Yearling Chinook salmon (*Oncorhynchus tshawytscha*)
Forebay	Area of Columbia River from McNary Dam to 2 km upstream.
NOAA Fisheries	National Oceanic and Atmospheric Administration National Marine Fisheries Service.
PIT	Passive integrated transponder.
Powerhouse	Turbine and Bypass (units 1–14).
rkm	River kilometer.
SOC	Sockeye salmon (*Oncorhynchus nerka*).
Spillway	Conventional spill bays (bays 1-22 excluding bays 19 and 20 in 2008 and 4 and 20 in 2009).
STH	Steelhead (*Oncorhynchus mykiss*).
Tailrace	Area of Columbia River from McNary Dam to 2.4 km downstream.
TSW	Temporary Spillway Weir.
USACE	United States Army Corps of Engineers.
USGS	United States Geological Survey.

Appendix A: Tagged Fish Characteristics for 2008–09

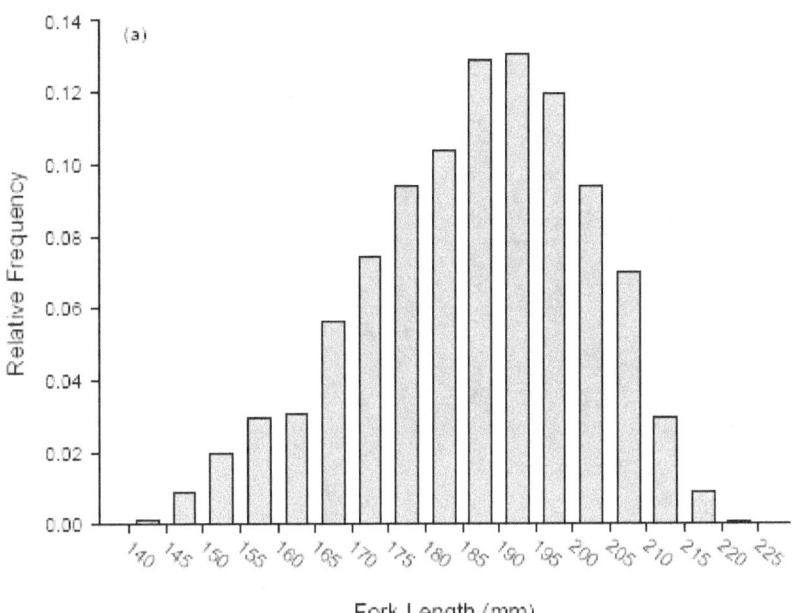

Figure A1. Graph showing fish length distribution of acoustic tagged juvenile steelhead released by Grant Public Utilities District in 2008 (from Sullivan and others, 2008).

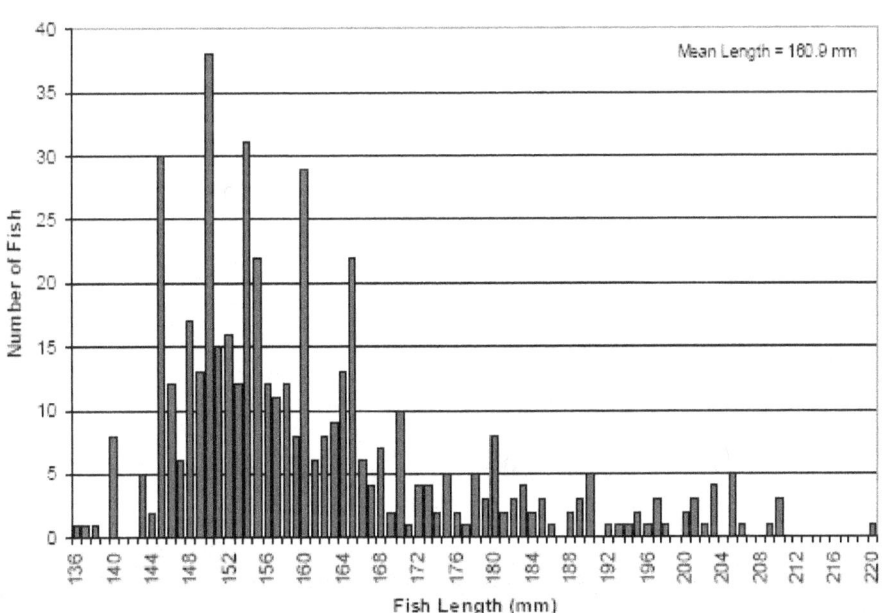

Figure A2. Graph showing fish length distribution of acoustic tagged yearling Chinook salmon released at Rocky Reach Dam in 2008 (from Steig and others, 2009).

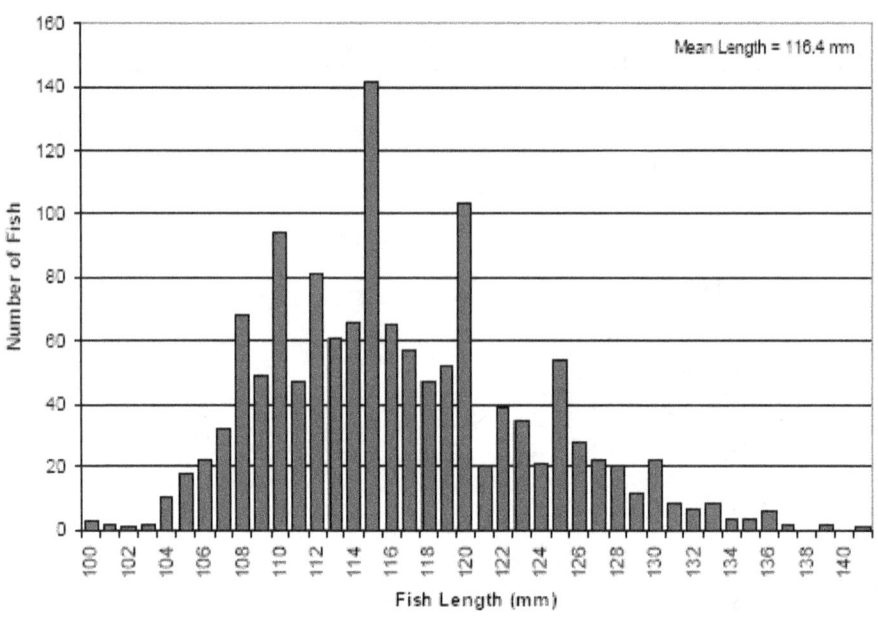

Figure A3. Graph showing fish length distribution of acoustic tagged sockeye salmon released at Wells and Rocky Reach Dam in 2008 (from Steig and others, 2009).

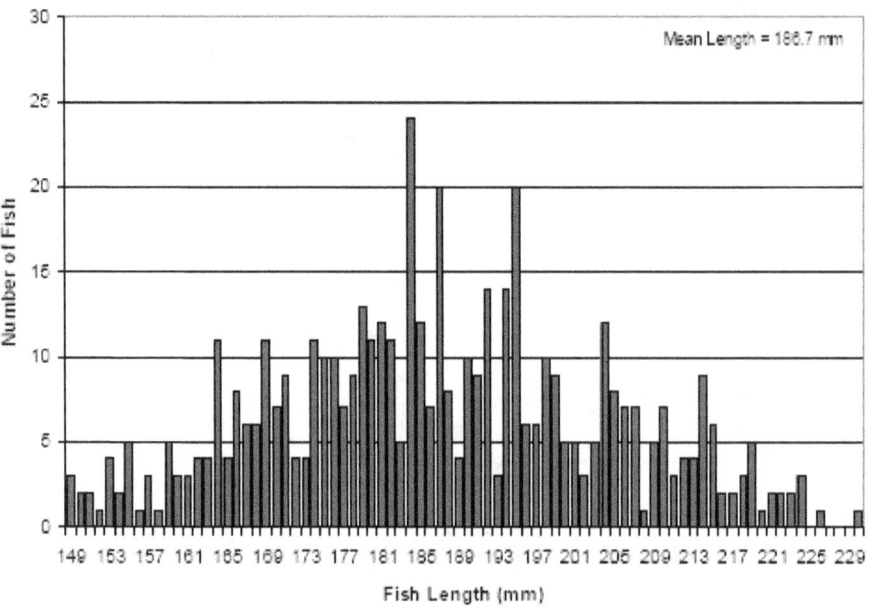

Figure A4. Graph showing fish length distribution of acoustic tagged juvenile steelhead released at Rocky Reach Dam in 2008 (from Steig and others, 2009).

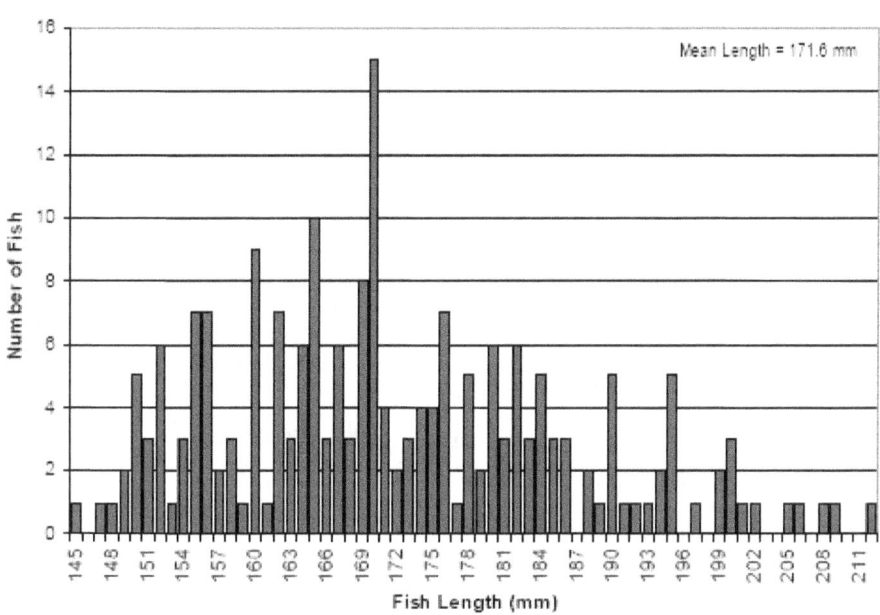

Figure A5. Graph showing fish length distribution of acoustic tagged yearling Chinook salmon released at Rocky Reach Dam in 2009 (from Steig and others, 2010).

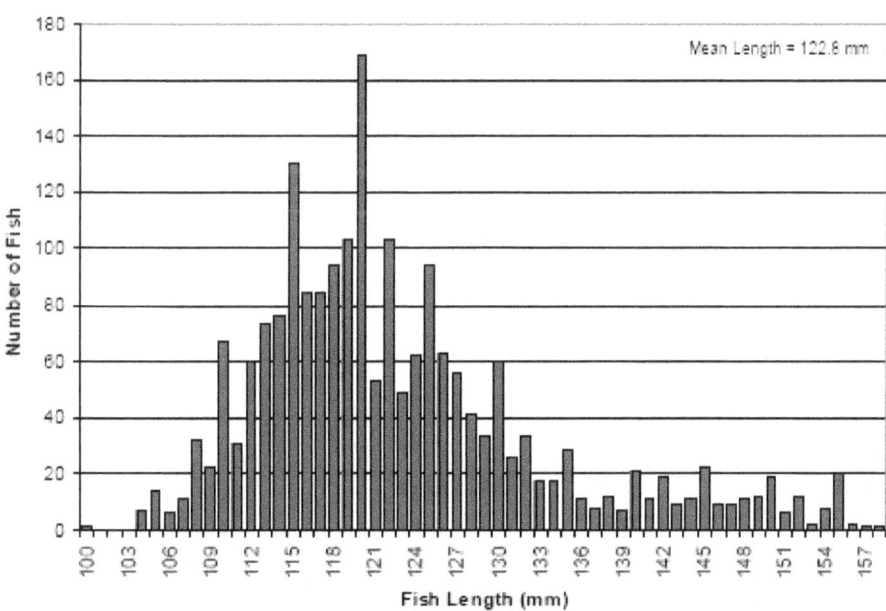

Figure A6. Graph showing fish length distribution of acoustic tagged sockeye salmon released at Wells and Rocky Reach Dam in 2009 (from Steig and others, 2010).

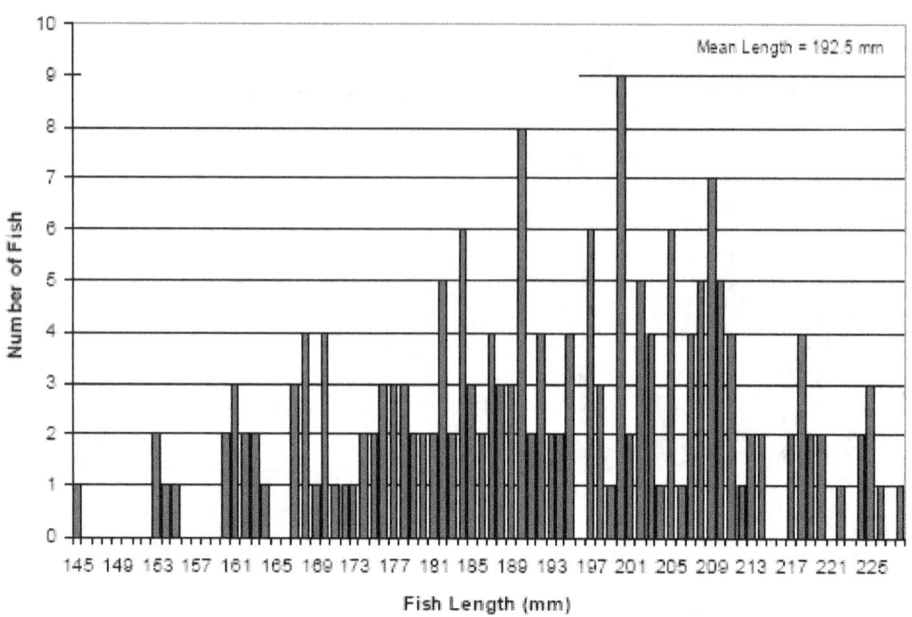

Figure A7. Graph showing fish length distribution of acoustic tagged juvenile steelhead released at Rocky Reach Dam in 2009 (from Steig and others, 2010).

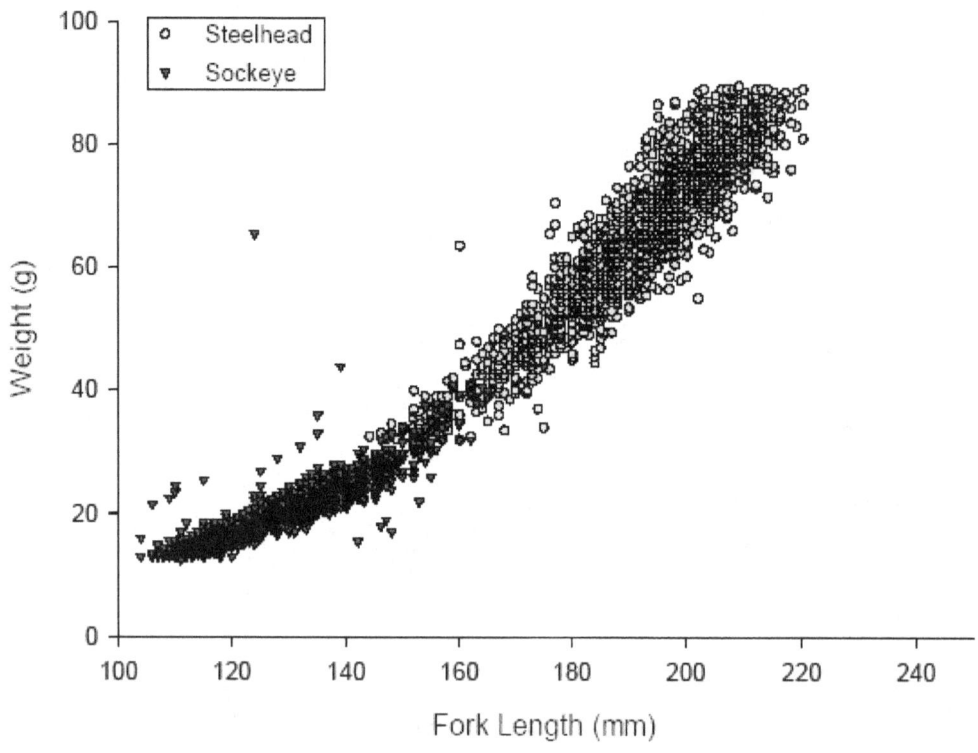

Figure A8. Graph showing size distribution of tagged juvenile steelhead (n = 2,093) and sockeye salmon (n = 1,941) that were released for the 2009 Grant PUD survival analysis (from Timko and others, 2010).

Appendix B: Goodness-of-Fit Test Results for the Route-Specific Survival Model used for Mid-Columbia River Released Fish Passing McNary Dam, 2008–09

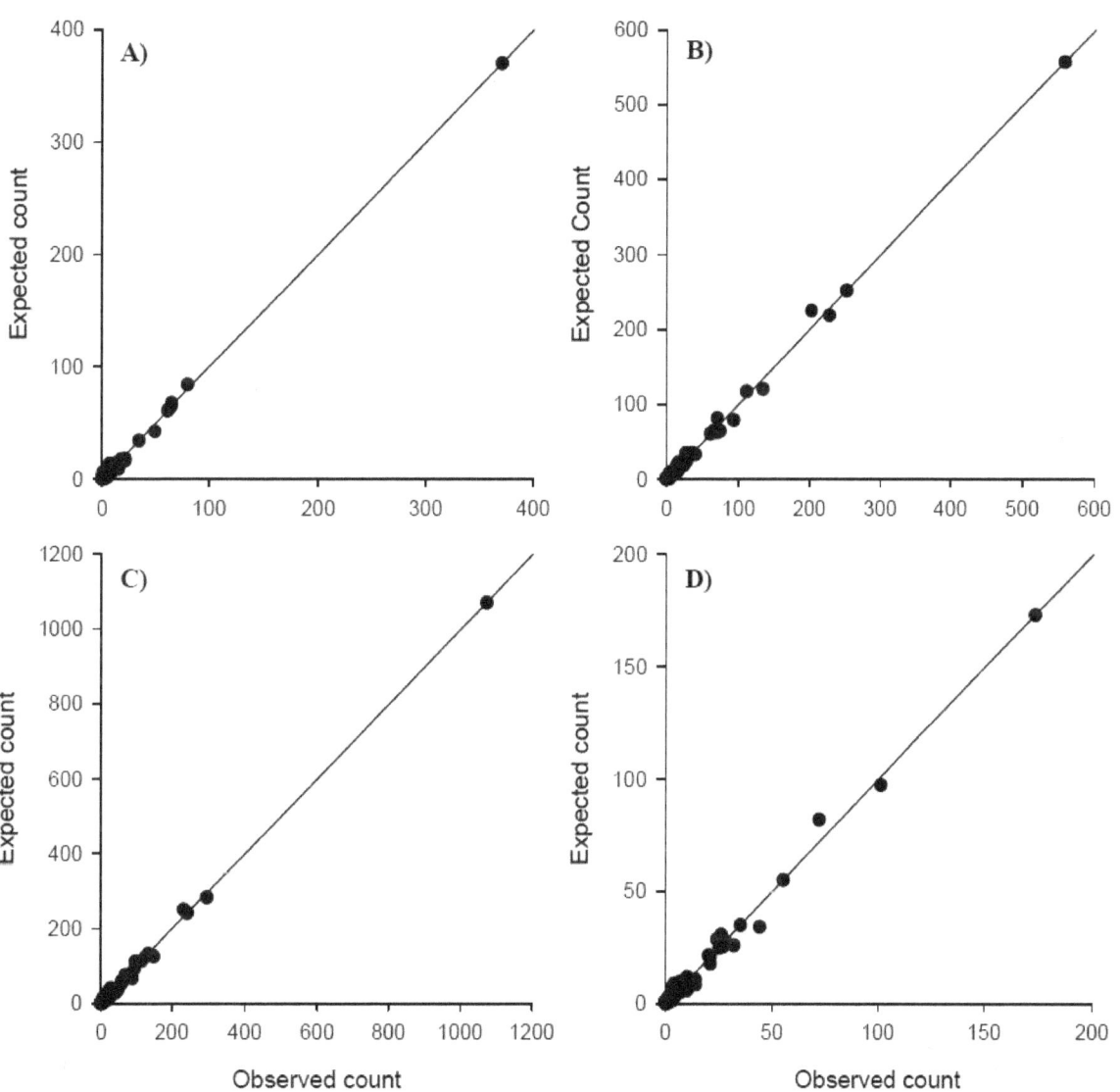

Figure B1. Graphs showing observed versus expected counts for the route-specific survival model of passage and survival of (*A*) yearling Chinook salmon, (*B*) sockeye salmon, (*C*) juvenile steelhead, and (*D*) juvenile steelhead also implanted with a PIT tag allowing use of a route-specific survival model with five routes , at McNary Dam for fish released in the Mid-Columbia River during spring 2008. The lines in plots are the 1:1 line.

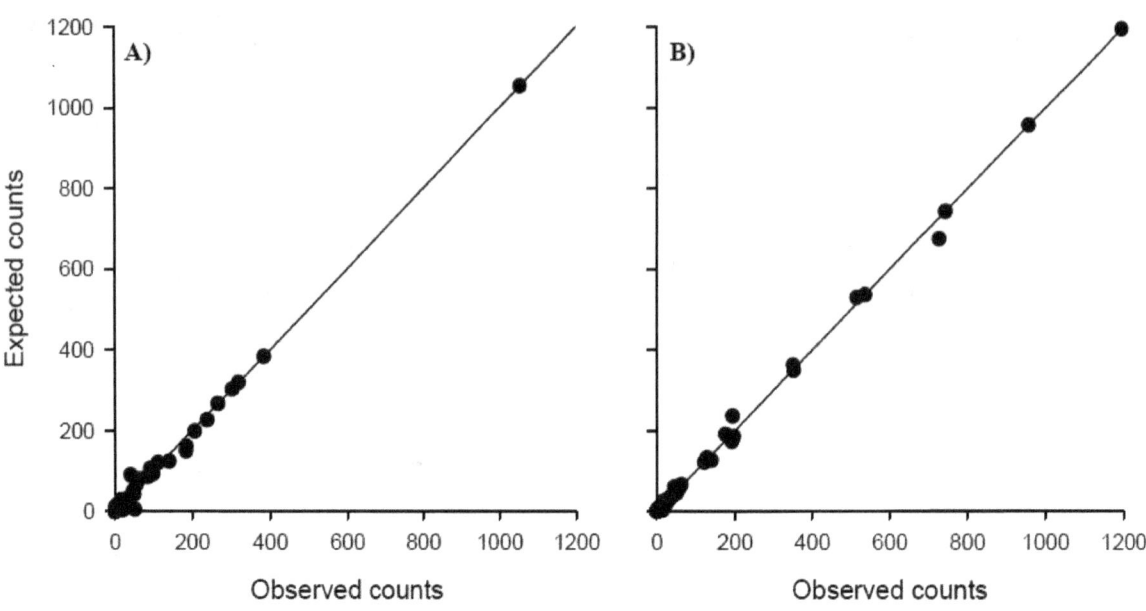

Figure B2. Graphs showing observed versus expected counts for the route-specific survival model of passage and survival of (A) juvenile steelhead and (B) sockeye salmon at McNary Dam for fish released in the Mid-Columbia River during spring 2009. The lines in plots are the 1:1 line.

Appendix C: Tag-Life Study for Mid-Columbia River Released Fish, 2008–09

Introduction

Tag-life studies were conducted in order to test assumption (7) of the survival model; that all tags are correctly identified and marks are not lost during the study. In the case of acoustic telemetry, when a transmitter fails the mark essentially is lost. Significant premature failure of transmitters can negatively bias survival estimates because survival models will interpret tag failure as mortality. However, if the rate of tag failure is known, survival estimates can be adjusted to correct for tag failure (Townsend and others, 2006; Cowen and Schwartz, 2005). Therefore, it is important to conduct a tag-life study as a measure of insurance. If a tag-life study is not conducted, little recourse is available for accurately adjusting survival estimates after conducting a study and finding that tags failed prematurely. Premature tag failure may occur through a number of mechanisms including batch-specific manufacturer defects or long travel times of fish due to low flows. Thus, it is important to conduct a tag-life study using a random sub-sample of transmitters that will be implanted in fish to test their performance under ambient field conditions during the study period. We used the methods of Townsend and others (2006) to achieve the following goals of the tag-life study (1) to estimate the probability that a tag was active at any point in time after it was turned on, (2) to estimate the probability of tags being in the study area at any given point in time after release, and (3) to estimate the average probability of a tag being active when passing telemetry arrays used for survival analysis. Given this information, we then determined whether the tag failure rate was high enough to warrant correction of survival estimates.

Methods

The tag-life studies conducted in 2008 and 2009 by Grant County Public Utilities District and Chelan County Public Utilities District were incorporated to estimate the tag life of transmitters implanted in yearling Chinook salmon, juvenile steelhead, and sockeye salmon. Tag-life studies in 2008 evaluated 100 model 795E and 51 model 795m transmitters. In 2009, 50 model 795E and 107 model 795m transmitters were evaluated for tag life.

Next, we estimated the probability of a tag being active at any given point in time. The lifetime of each tag was calculated as the elapsed time between the time a tag was turned on and the time that the last detection was recorded by the data logging receiver. We then fit a survival distribution function to the tag-life data to estimate the probability of a tag operating for a given amount of time. Although many forms of survival distribution functions can be fit to this data, we chose to use the Kaplan-Meier distribution because this distribution fits the tag-life data well. The Kaplan-Meier survival distribution function takes the form:

$$S(t) = \Pr\{T > t\} \qquad\qquad (C1)$$

where $S(t)$ is the probability of a tag surviving to time t.

We used maximum likelihood methods to fit the Kaplan-Meier survival distribution function to the empirical survival distribution function. The empirical survival distribution function is the proportion of tags surviving to time t.

The probability that a tag is active when it arrives at a detection array is dependent on the travel time of the tag to each detection array used in the survival analysis. For the route specific survival model, the travel times of interest are from time of release to the time of detection at McNary Dam, from time of release to the time of detection at first downstream gate, and from the time of release to the time of first detection at any one of the remaining downstream arrays used for survival analysis. In addition to fish travel time, the travel time of the tag must include all elapsed time that the transmitter was operating prior to fish release. Therefore, the duration of time from activation to release was calculated and added to the travel time of fish to each detection array. We then plotted the empirical cumulative travel time distribution, which is the proportion of fish arriving at a given detection array at time t, against the survival distribution function, to understand whether most fish passed the detection arrays prior to tag failure.

To quantify the rate of tag failure we calculated the average probability that the tag was active for the ith release group to the jth detection array (Townsend and others, 2006):

$$\hat{P}(L_{ij}) = \frac{1}{k_{ij}} \sum_{x=1}^{k_{ij}} \hat{S}(t_{ijx})$$

(C2)

Where $\hat{P}(L_{ij})$ = average probability that a tag is active at the jth detection array from the ith release group.

$\hat{S}(h_{ijx})$ = the estimated probability that a tag is active at time t_{ijx} for the xth fish arriving at the jth detection array for the ith release group. $\hat{S}(h_{ijx})$ is calculated by plugging into the survival distribution function the travel time of each tag to each detection array.

k_{ij} = the total number of fish detected at the jth detection array for the ith release group.

Results and Discussion

The tag-life data showed the tag failure range for model 795E transmitters to be from 4.3 to 42.6 days in 2008 and from 6.0 to 49.0 days in 2009. The tag failure range for model 795m transmitters was from 3.5 to 19.5 days in 2008 and 4.9 to 30.5 days in 2009. The mean operational life of model 795E transmitters was 20.9 days and 26.4 days for 2008 and 2009, respectively. The model 795m transmitter mean operational life was 15.7 days for 2008 and 19.5 days for 2009 (table C1). The overall timing of tag failure is depicted by the Kaplan-Meier survival distribution function (figs. C1 and C2).

Table C1. Descriptive statistics of transmitter life measured in days for transmitter model 795-E, used in yearling Chinook salmon and juvenile steelhead and model 795-m, used in sockeye salmon during 2008–09.

Transmitter type	Number of tags	Mean tag life	Standard deviation	Minimum tag life	Maximum tag life
2008 795E	100	20.9	5.2	4.3	42.6
2008 795m	51	15.7	3.7	3.5	19.5
2009 795E	50	26.4	7.2	6.0	49.0
2009 795m	107	19.5	4.9	4.9	30.5

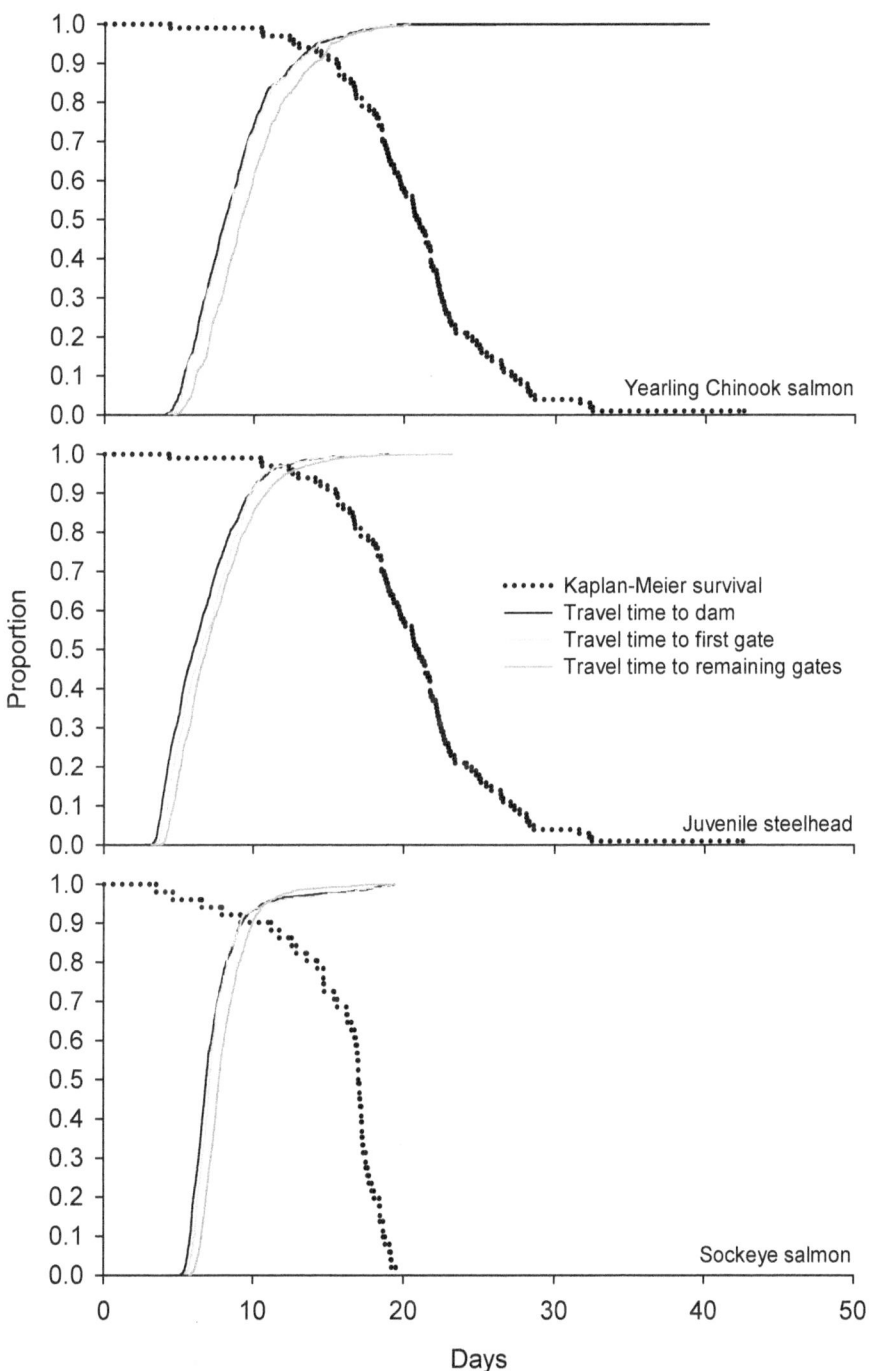

Figure C1. Graphs showing travel time distributions of transmitters compared to the survival distribution function for transmitter battery life of Mid-Columbia acoustic-tagged salmonids at McNary Dam, 2008. Travel time distributions include the total elapsed time that the transmitter was operating prior to release of the fish. Cumulative travel times for yearling Chinook salmon and juvenile steelhead are compared to the survival distribution for model 795E transmitters. Cumulative travel time for sockeye salmon are compared to the survival distribution for model 795m transmitters.

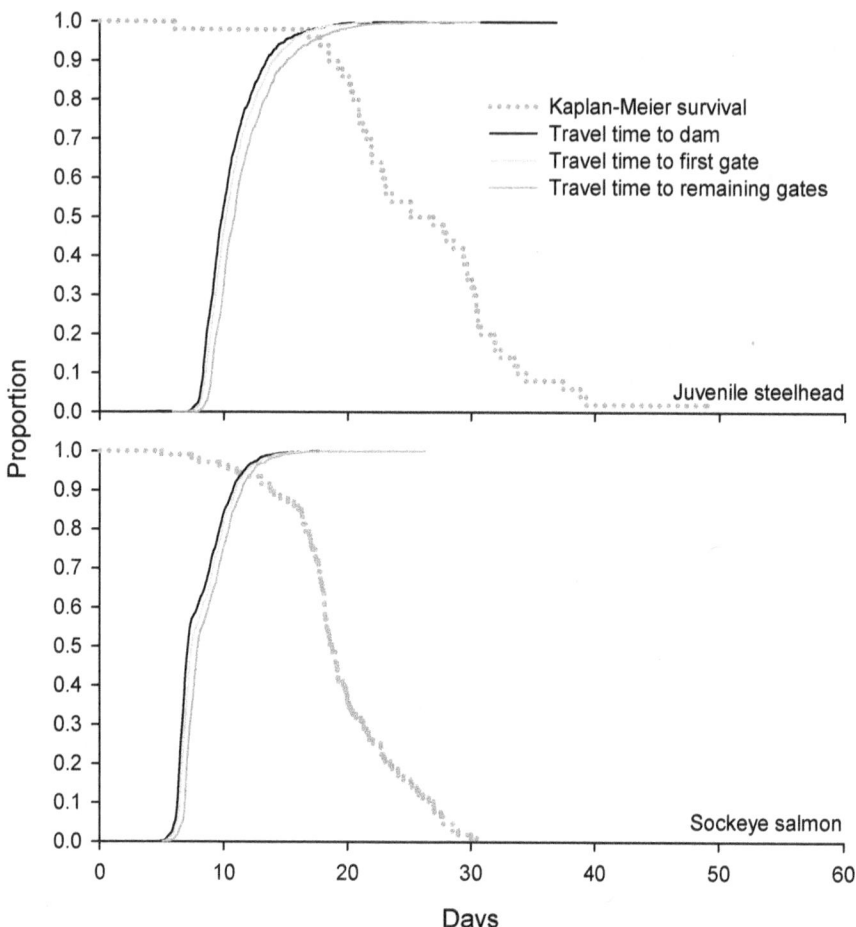

Figure C2. Graphs showing travel time distributions of transmitters compared to the survival distribution function for transmitter battery life of Mid-Columbia acoustic-tagged salmonids at McNary Dam, 2009. Travel time distributions include the total elapsed time that the transmitter was operating prior to release of the fish. Cumulative travel times for juvenile steelhead are compared to the survival distribution for model 795E transmitters. Cumulative travel times for sockeye salmon are compared to the survival distribution for model 795 m transmitters.

The comparison of cumulative travel times from release to the detection arrays and the survival distribution function resulted in relatively high probabilities of the transmitters being operational when the fish reached the arrays (figs. C1 and C2; table C2). For both 2008 and 2009, the cumulative travel times from release to the detection arrays are approaching probabilities (97–99 percent) where bias would be a concern for yearling Chinook salmon and juvenile steelhead. Sockeye salmon travel times in 2008 are close to introducing bias to the survival estimate with a 92 percent probability of the transmitters being operational at the arrays. Travel times for sockeye salmon in 2009 show increased probabilities of transmitters being operational, up to a probability of 97 percent, but these travel times are still borderline for being a concern for potential bias (table C2).

Townsend and others (2006) found that the adjusted survival estimates (0.9387) changed very little from the unadjusted estimate (0.9339) when the probability of a tag being operational at downstream detection arrays was high (greater than 98). Cowen and Schwarz (2005) found that survival estimates that do not account for tag failure have potential to be biased, especially when failure rates exceed 10 percent. Our tag failure rates were between 1 and 3 percent for all fish except sockeye salmon in 2008 (which still had a tag failure rate less than 10 percent). We feel that the variance was high enough for uncorrected survival estimates that correcting the variance using the tag life data would be inconsequential. We conclude that this is likely true even for the high probability of tag failure occurring for the 2008 sockeye salmon, because this was a relatively small data set and the variance about these estimates are relatively high.

Table C2. Mean probability of transmitters being operational [$\hat{P}(L_{ij})$] when passing telemetry detection sites used in the survival study conducted at McNary Dam, 2008–09.

Species	Detection site	Mean	Standard deviation
	2008		
Chinook salmon	McNary Dam	0.977	0.053
	First detection site downstream of McNary Dam	0.977	0.040
	Second, third, and fourth detection sites downstream of McNary Dam	0.970	0.050
Juvenile steelhead	McNary Dam	0.989	0.019
	First detection site downstream of McNary Dam	0.989	0.017
	Second, third, and fourth detection sites downstream of McNary Dam	0.984	0.037
Sockeye salmon	McNary Dam	0.927	0.101
	First detection site downstream of McNary Dam	0.924	0.101
	Second, 3rd, third, and fourth detection sites downstream of McNary Dam	0.926	0.049
	2009		
Juvenile steelhead	McNary Dam	0.978	0.029
	First detection site downstream of McNary Dam	0.978	0.018
	Second, third, and fourth detection sites downstream of McNary Dam	0.973	0.042
Sockeye salmon	McNary Dam	0.978	0.021
	First detection site downstream of McNary Dam	0.975	0.025
	Second, third, and fourth detection sites downstream of McNary Dam	0.971	0.033